Winning Ways

PHILIP JINADU

Philip Jinadu has been involved in evangelistic ministry for over twenty years. After a number of years working as a National Evangelist with Youth for Christ, he transitioned into local church leadership within the Pioneer stream of churches. In 2001 Philip was invited to move to Bristol by a network of church leaders to pioneer and fulfil a role as a City Evangelist. This led to the creation of the evangelistic agency, ICQ, and the development of the Winning Ways process for long-term church growth.

Philip now works with a huge cross section of churches from every denomination. As well as a number of evangelistic equipping courses, Philip has written *Up Close and Personal*, a discipleship primer for new Christians.

DAVID LAWRENCE

David Lawrence has over eighteen years' experience of local church leadership. The church he served as leader enjoyed consistent growth, starting from a handful of people and finishing with over three hundred. He has also been involved with several church planting projects within the UK. He is a local tutor for the MA in Missional Leadership course run by Birmingham Christian College/Together in Mission, and holds an MTh in Applied Theology and an MA in Consultancy for Mission and Ministry. His other books include *The Chocolate Teapot* (for young people) and *Heaven; It's Not the End of the World*.

Winning Ways

*How to Create a Culture of Outreach
in your Church*

Philip Jinadu and David Lawrence

Authentic

LONDON • COLORADO SPRINGS • HYDERABAD

First published 2007 by Authentic Media
9 Holdom Avenue, Bletchley, Milton Keynes, Bucks, MK1 1QR, UK
1820 Jet Stream Drive, Colorado Springs, CO 80921, USA
OM Authentic Media, Medchal Road, Jeedimetla Village,
Secunderabad 500 055, A.P., India

www.authenticmedia.co.uk

Authentic Media is a division of IBS-STL UK,
a company limited by guarantee (registered charity no. 270162)

British Library Cataloguing in Publication Data
A catalogue record for this book is available from the British Library

ISBN-13: 978-1-85078-738-9
ISBN-10: 1-85078-738-7

Cover Design by MOOSE77
Print Management by Adare Carwin
Typeset by Waverley Typesetters, Fakenham
Printed and bound in Great Britain by J.H. Haynes & Co., Sparkford

Dedication

The material in this book has been developed in real, live churches over a number of years. Our insights have come as we have tried to serve and work alongside many different leaders and ministries. The ideas and models that we have formulated have been largely provoked, practised and proved by them.

They are part of an army of dedicated, passionate leaders who are seeking to serve the church and extend the kingdom in this nation, sometimes in challenging situations, often with little reward.

It is to these servants of Christ that we dedicate this book.

PHILIP JINADU and DAVID LAWRENCE
Bristol 2007

Contents

Contents

PART ONE

Creating a Culture of Outreach
Getting the CONTENT right

PHILIP JINADU

Chapter 1

Evangelistic Leadership

> 'The pessimist complains about the wind. The optimist
> expects it to change. The leader adjusts the sails.'
>
> John Maxwell[1]

It started with a brother and sister.

Jenny became a Christian in her mid-thirties; Mark, her
brother, was a self-made businessman, not interested in
faith or the church. Jenny spent the next six years trying
to share her faith with Mark. She learnt the four spiritual
laws, she prayed as much as she could, she invited Mark
to church meetings and events repeatedly. All without
success.

On one level Jenny and Mark were close; on another,
worlds apart. Jenny was passionate about her faith, but
unable to draw her brother in; Mark was indulgent of his
sister's new interests, happy if she was happy, but utterly
uninterested himself. In other words, they typified the
church and the UK population as a whole.

For him, church was irrelevant, all invitations to look
closer were swatted politely aside. For her, faith sharing

---

[1]   John C. Maxwell, *The 21 Irrefutable Laws of Leadership* (Nashville, TN:
Thomas Nelson, 1998).

was frustrating, prayer was disheartening, and outreach wasn't working.

Then Jenny's home group began examining principles of lifestyle outreach. They began to support each other in their personal outreach, praying together and sharing stories. They began to see themselves, and their Christ-centred community experience, as a sign that needed to be seen by those on the outside. They began to look differently at outreach, finding new but natural ways to throw open the doors of their faith community. In simple ways, almost without realizing it, they began to create a culture of outreach.

And that was how Jenny got to invite Mark and his family to join in on a home group camping weekend. Actually, it was a trip to a Christian music festival, but Mark and his family came anyway. Mark didn't go to any of the Christian meetings, but nonetheless something profound began to happen. In the midst of campfire chat and baking beans, Mark started to find himself drawn irresistibly to this group of friends. There was something about them that he found utterly attractive.

The next Sunday Mark was in church, sitting on the front row with his wife and three children.

Mark said that he came simply because he wanted to meet up with the great friends that he'd made on holiday. Without awaiting invitation, he came the next week. And then the next. At the end of that third Sunday meeting he found himself breaking down in tears. As one, the home group gathered round him and gently led him to Christ.

Over the next year or so, half a dozen other people came to faith through that little home group, including Mark's wife and cousin. That group of ten ordinary Christians, who'd gone for years without seeing a single person come to faith, suddenly found themselves in the middle of something. It wasn't the Welsh Revival, but it was tremendously exciting just the same. And it spread out and affected other groups in the church.

Imagine that you were seeing that kind of natural, organic growth happening consistently, right across the board in your church. Imagine if that was the norm. It's easy to see isolated pockets of growth like that in a church, but imagine how it would be if the whole body got in on the act. Imagine what it would be like if forty year old businessmen were regularly coming to faith in your ordinary services. Imagine if outreach was a consistent, natural value that worked itself out in a myriad of un-anticipated ways in your church.

In many ways Jenny's story exemplifies what we all want to see: ordinary people coming to faith in churches that are geared up for a continuous process of making and nurturing disciples of Jesus Christ. The reality is, however, that across the UK church scene, this story is far from typical.

Facing reality

As is now well known, statistics paint a depressing picture of the UK church. We have a future. It just seems a bleak one.

For the last few decades the British church has been in numerical decline. Back in 1979 about 12 per cent of the entire population could be found in church on a Sunday. By 2005 this had plummeted to 6.3 per cent.[2] According to research published in the *Daily Telegraph*, around ten churches in the UK close every week. If

---

[2] Dr Peter Brierley (ed), *Pulling out of the Nosedive* and *Religious Trends No 6 2006/2007* (London: Christian Research, 2006).

trends continue, by 2040 those attending church on a Sunday will account for just 2 per cent of the population – half the number attending mosque on a Friday – and the average age of the church member will be sixty-four years old.[3]

I have nothing against sixty-four year olds, but it's not a tremendously exciting picture.

There are some positives. Whilst small churches are getting smaller, and many are disappearing all together, a good proportion of large churches are getting a little larger.[4] Recent statistics indicate that the decline is less severe than it was back in the glory days of the 90s. (Remember how, during the Decade of Evangelism, the British church *lost* over a million members?) Nationally, Black-Majority churches are growing nicely, to the point that white Christians in inner-city London are now the minority, church-wise.[5]

It's not all disastrous news, by any means. Some of it is merely discouraging.

To borrow a phrase from the environmental lobby, what we have here is 'an inconvenient truth.' However you read the statistics, there is an unavoidable issue here. And it's not clear that things are going to get any better. The issue is not global warming, but national cooling. There's a cooling in the credibility of the church. There's a cooling in people coming to faith in Christ. And there's a cooling in the Christian confidence in the gospel.

---

[3] Christian Research, *Religious Trends No 5*, quoted in the *Daily Telegraph*, September 2005.

[4] One hundred out of 172 larger Anglican churches in the UK have grown by at least 1 per cent during the last twenty years – the majority of which are evangelical. The average congregation of larger churches has grown from 460 in 1989, to 490 in 1998, and is likely to become 590 by 2010.

[5] *Religious Trends No 6 2006/2007*, ibid.

A new type of leadership

We're writing this book because we believe there are answers. Clearly we believe there's hope. You're reading this book because you want to see a different future and you believe that you and your church have a part to play. Exciting days lie ahead. But the answers may not be what you expect.

When confronted with these questions, and facing this challenge, we often revert to what we know. We rationalize that what is needed is better, more effective evangelistic initiatives and programmes. We look for the next big thing, the one-size-fits-all strategy, the latest tried and tested technique. It's tempting to cast around, looking for evangelistic gifts that we can import into the church. If we can get the right gifted people with some powerful new initiative, then things will move forward. Programmes and professionals will save us.

But that kind of thinking falls short. What we need is not more *evangelistic gift* in the church. The church is awash with evangelistic gift and potential. It always has been, it always will be, even in the worst of decline.

And it's not about having more *evangelistic initiatives*, either – more events, more campaigns, more great ideas. They have their place. But the Decade of Evangelism, brimming with initiatives and programmes, ultimately only took us from declining to declining and exhausted.

No. The answer is leadership. Little surprise there, perhaps. But it's the *type* of leadership needed which is key. What we desperately need to rediscover is *evangelistic leadership*.

Let's be clear. We're not saying that the only churches that have a chance of growing are the ones led by an evangelistically gifted leader. We're certainly not advocating that evangelists take over leadership of local churches. In fact, in many cases that would be a spectacularly bad idea. What we *are* advocating, though, is a leadership style, a leadership philosophy, a leadership emphasis. It's a type of leadership that needs to pervade every level of church life, from the core to the grass roots.

Evangelistic leadership creates a culture of outreach. Evangelistic leadership understands the nature of church and the principles of outreach. It builds something long-term, holistic and effective. Evangelistic leadership is the only thing that can effectively unlock the enormous growth potential of the local church. It is the powerful synthesis of the gifts and ministry of the pastor and the evangelist.

In many churches this is a novel idea. Take the case of Bill, who recently accepted a teaching post at a major denominational ministry training college in America. He was the kind of person that you could sit and listen to for ages, such was his wealth of experience and knowledge of Scripture. The college which he had joined had many hundreds of students and a teaching faculty of nearly sixty academics.

However, as Bill got to know his new colleagues he discovered that not one of them had led a church where anyone at all had come to faith in Christ. Think about that for a moment. A whole generation of church leaders being trained by people who themselves had never experienced leading someone to faith.

This may be an extreme example, but it is not untypical. Many church leaders have never received training in leading outward focused, missional churches. Many leaders have themselves come from churches that rarely see people come to faith.

This book is for church leaders everywhere who long to see people in their communities, and in the friendship networks of their members, come to faith in Jesus. It's not for high-flying superstar leaders of mega-churches. This is evangelistic leadership for the rest of us. It's for those who may not see themselves as evangelists, but nonetheless have an evangelistic concern to reach the lost, the last and the least.

This is our creed

We're writing this book because we want to see people of all ages and backgrounds discover a living relationship with their Father in heaven. If you want that too, keep reading.

We have a few core beliefs related to that desire that have spurred us to write this book for you. It may help you get a feel for where we are headed if we list them here

- We believe that the God of everywhere and everyone is involved in a passionate search for his estranged children, and that he invites those of us who already have been happily reunited with him (the church) to join him in that search.

- We believe that the gospel and Christian mission is about more than seeing individuals reconciled to God; *but we believe that it is never less than that.* In 1988 the Lambeth Conference of the Anglican Church identified the following five marks of the church's mission:[6]

  - To proclaim the good news of the kingdom.
  - To teach, baptize and nurture new believers.

---

[6] Anglican Consultative Council, *The Official Report of the Lambeth Conference 1998: Transformation and Renewal* (Harrisburg, PA: Morehouse Publishing, 1999).

- To respond to human need by loving service.
- To seek to transform unjust structures in society.
- To strive to safeguard the integrity of creation and sustain and renew the earth.

We fully endorse all of these activities as legitimate expressions of the church's mission, but in this book we are focusing on the interface between the first and second of these 'marks.' Specifically we are addressing the question, 'How can local churches proclaim the good news of the kingdom in such a way that there will constantly be new believers who require teaching, baptizing and nurturing coming to faith?'

- We believe that evangelism is what happens when people who love Jesus, love those around them. It is not an extra 'church' activity; rather it is the natural overflow of authentic everyday discipleship.

- We believe that healthy churches will naturally attract people to Jesus.

- We believe that effective structures and strategic planning are vital to fulfilling a church's outreach potential.

- We believe that every church has key people with evangelistic gifts and motivation – you need to find and develop them.

- We believe that the ministries of the evangelist and the pastor-teacher are key to the empowerment of the church for evangelistic fruitfulness.

If you share our beliefs, but are maybe struggling to work out how they make sense in your local church situation, then this book is for you. We want to lead you through a process of exploring these beliefs and working out their implications and applications in your local church.

But first let's unpack that last point a little and give a bit of biographical background to the principles and teaching to come.

Smarter than the average bear

The well-known story of the pastor and evangelist who go on a retreat together illustrates some popular perceptions of those two ministries. Having reached their remote cabin in the woods they settle for a night's sleep. The following morning the pastor wakes up to discover the evangelist has disappeared. As he gets up to find out where his colleague has gone, the pastor hears frantic shouting from outside the cabin. He looks out of the window and sees the evangelist running for his life down the hill towards the cabin, pursued by a huge grizzly bear. As they approach the cabin the bear is gaining on the evangelist, who is now screaming for the pastor to open the door, open the door!

As the evangelist gets to the door the pastor throws it open, whereupon the evangelist deftly swerves to the right and the bear, which is right behind him by now, lumbers straight into the cabin.

As the alarmed and now-cornered pastor takes rapid stock of the situation he sees through the open door the evangelist running back up the hill and hears him call over his shoulder: 'You look after that one. I'll go catch some more!'

The evangelist is the unpredictable lone hunter who has the courage and skill to lure the unsuspecting into a trap, whilst the pastor is the stay-at-home type who 'looks after' people, and picks up the pieces after the evangelist has left for another trip.

This may be a caricature but it is one that can be all too near to the truth.

New models and new connections

In the early years of my ministry I probably did my fair share of 'bear hunting.' As an itinerant evangelist I got to work with scores of different churches. I was involved with missions and crusades and other high profile evangelistic initiatives. There was plenty of good fruit and positive impact. But there was often disappointment that churches didn't seem to grow over the long-term in proportion to the effects and excitement we'd generated in the short-term.

If pastors were shocked by us evangelists flinging the front door wide open to usher in bears, then we for our part were often shocked to discover months later that the back door had been left wide open too. Our bears were back in the woods, and the churches were back at square one.

The turning point for me came when I took a sideways step into local church leadership. For seven years I helped lead a large church in the south of England, and it was here that I began to grapple with the issue of evangelism and the local church. I discovered that the brief training that I'd been giving churches to prepare them for outreach and mission wasn't exactly wrong. But it wasn't that simple, either.

Having spent valuable and formative years working out the role of the evangelist in local church, exploring the building blocks of a culture of outreach, and developing models of evangelistic leadership, I found myself called into a new role. From 2001 I was invited to pioneer a regional ministry in the south-west as a 'City Evangelist.'

Working these principles through over the long-term with many different churches has been tremendously encouraging. It's been the most exciting and fruitful period of ministry that I've ever experienced, and a major reason for that success has come through partnership with one of the local leaders, David Lawrence.

David spent eighteen years as the pastor of a church, seeing it grow from three people to three hundred. Even more impressive, approximately half of that growth came from people coming to faith. Our partnership began as I worked alongside his church as an evangelist, preaching, teaching and training. It then developed as he stepped down from leadership to take up a wider role, including joining my regional team as a senior church consultant.

Two halves

In many ways David lived out and embodied the principles of evangelistic leadership. Although not an evangelist himself, he managed to lead with evangelistic insight and values, and to build evangelistic structures and strategy into church life.

Evangelism cannot be simply bolted on to a local church. It has to be pervasive, cultural and organic. It takes evangelistic leadership and the release of natural evangelistic gifts at the grass roots of church to achieve this.

So it's not only our belief, but also our experience that *when the gift of the evangelist and the gift of the pastor-teacher operate in partnership to create a culture of outreach within a local church, evangelistic fruitfulness inevitably follows.* The goal of this book is to explain, defend and amplify that claim so that churches of all sorts in all situations find that they are marked by the regular need to 'teach, baptize and nurture new believers.'

The book itself is a product of the pastor/evangelist partnership. It's a distillation of the work that we now do with churches in order to create effective, sustainable

growth. In this first half I, as an evangelist, will tackle the
content of a culture of outreach. I'll look at the principles
of outreach, the mobilization of members in ministry, the
engagement of evangelistic gift at the grass roots and the
creation of the outreach culture.

In the second half David, as a pastor, will tackle
the *context* of a culture of outreach. He'll look at the
fundamental issues of church health that every leader has
to address in order to make sure that, at the very least, the
back door stays shut. He'll lay out a template for healthy
church, and explore how to develop the life of the church
so that a culture of outreach can thrive.

Finally, we'll provide some simple tools for strategic
planning and a joined-up approach to the outreach
process.

Taking things further

We have good news and bad news for you. The good news
is that we can offer you some tried and tested principles
that have been successfully piloted, honed and developed
over a number of years in a number of different styles of
church.

The bad news is that putting these principles into
action is still going to be an enormously challenging and
demanding exercise. There is no quick fix here.

We can give you all of the principles and a lot of
the practice, but we can't give you all of the answers.
It's not within the scope of this one book to provide
a comprehensive primer for all the intricacies of the
outreach process in your church. You're going to have to
work out some of this for yourself.

We can offer you two things, though.

First, we can help you talk things through with your
leadership team. We may not have the space to give you

all the answers, but we can at least provide you with some of the major questions. At the end of each chapter that follows, we'll lay out some basic questions for discussion. You may want to read this book as a leadership team, as well as drawing in key movers and shakers.

You could engage with the material as a team by reading a chapter a week, meeting to discuss the questions before moving on to the next chapter. Giving the first half hour or so of a regular team meeting to look through some of these key questions could make a profound investment in your leadership together. Alternatively, you may want to use the questions to guide a special leadership retreat, or simply to inform your own thinking about church.

However you do it, wrestling with the end of chapter questions should help earth the principles in this book, and translate them into a workable reality for your church.

Secondly, we can point you to further resources. In our work with churches over the last six years we've developed many teaching and training resources. We've created leadership consultations, online health audits, internet podcasts, a DVD library of teaching, and a number of training and equipping courses. We've detailed some of these in the Appendices at the end of the book. You may want to use these to help you access these resources, or simply to provide ideas and a starting-point for your own in-house teaching and resources.

But for now, let's begin with the basic material.

It's our conviction that the local church is still the best agency for outreach and community transformation. The good news is still good news. Our prayer is that God would inspire, equip and enable you as you read, in order that you might develop evangelistic leadership and a culture of outreach in a church that is growing in health, maturity and salvation.

Chapter 2

What is a Culture of Outreach?

'Failing to understand how culture works is just as
dangerous in the organizational world as failing to
understand gravity and the atmosphere in the physical
world.'

Edgar H. Schein[1]

Here's an interesting thing.

If you take a mug of steaming hot coffee and place
it in a fridge, two things will happen. First of all, in a
small but very real way, the temperature of that fridge,
and everything in it, will rise. The coffee is hot, and will
make a short-term difference to its environment. Energy is
released, things change, there's movement and impact.

But then the second thing happens. After a small and
one-sided tussle, the fridge cools the coffee. Ten minutes
later, everything is as it was.

It's called thermodynamics. Which is a fancy way of
saying you can't beat the system.

Culture is the fundamental system in your church. It's
the basic nature, the prevailing conditions, the essential
personality of a church. Or in the words of the late Bishop

---

[1] Edgar H. Schein, *Organizational Culture and Leadership* (San Francisco,
    CA: Jossey-Bass, 1991), p. 48.

of Liverpool, Derek Worlock, 'Culture is the way we do things round here.'

So many church evangelistic programmes amount to little more than putting cups of coffee in the fridge. They essentially import an event, or an initiative, a meeting, a programme, a training course, a speaker into a church system – but without fundamentally addressing the *nature* of that system. You get a short term impact, the evangelistic temperature of the church rises a notch, then the system inexorably fights back to restore the status quo.

Creating a culture of outreach is the only way to effectively deliver long-term, healthy growth. In a culture of outreach, growth happens naturally and inevitably. It's woven into the fabric of church life, embedded into the psyche. A culture of outreach doesn't depend on programmes and professionals, but focuses on people and process. Instead of an artificial 'bolt-on' extra, outreach becomes holistic, continuous and almost unconscious; growth is the natural, organic result.

Creating a culture of outreach means that we set about building an oven, instead of just tinkering about with the fridge.

How does your garden grow?

The root word for 'culture' comes from the Latin, *'culturare'*, which means to 'grow, nurture or tend.' It's the same root as for the word 'cultivate' and it's the source of the word 'agriculture' – literally, 'the tending of fields.' Culture is essentially the beliefs, values and behaviour that are cultivated in a group of people or in an organization.

For better or worse, your true values determine your culture and in turn, your culture nurtures, promotes and propagates those values. It doesn't matter what you say you believe, what information you teach or what knowledge you impart. Ultimately, behaviour results from the values that your culture naturally, albeit unconsciously, promotes.

You see cultures in organizations and families, as well as in larger sociological groups. A couple of years ago my wife, Kate, and I went to Egypt for a second honeymoon by the Red Sea. I was particularly struck by the culture of the hotel in which we were staying. It was a big, ostentatious number, part of a multinational, prestige chain. I expected the usual mix of snooty formality and dry efficiency.

But the minute we stepped into the foyer we encountered a wildly refreshing culture. It hit you faster than the air-conditioning. A tremendously keen and friendly manager materialized and escorted us to our room, throwing open the door and ushering us in, with a flourish. Next morning, at breakfast, Kate dropped her napkin on the floor, and before she could bend down to retrieve it, the world's most keen and friendly waiter rushed up and, with a flourish, presented her with a fresh one. Later that day I approached a gap-toothed gardener for directions, only to have him stop everything he was doing. Demonstrating breathtaking keenness and friendliness, he then escorted me to my destination. With a flourish.

That's what culture is. It's a pattern of thought and behaviour that has been bred into a group so completely that it becomes endemic. Like Blackpool rock, the values run right through every part of the organization, from top to bottom. It's who they are. Or rather, it's who they've become.

And you see it in churches, too. I visit my fair share of churches and I've seen that unconscious culture manifest itself in hundreds of different ways. Some churches are incredibly welcoming; others politely ignore you. Some churches are full of life and faith and energy; others give off a more defeated air. You see cultures of prayer, cultures of worship, cultures of social engagement. It may not always be apparent to those *in* the churches. But from the outside looking in, it's striking.

So what does a culture of outreach look like?

A new model of outreach

Most people looking for good models of outreach look either to the beginning of John's Gospel or to the beginning of Luke's sequel, Acts.

In John chapter 1 we see the archetypal picture of the classic *'individual soul-winner.'* There's an encouraging picture of John the Baptist's disciples becoming followers of Jesus. Andrew believes, then witnesses to his brother, Simon Peter. Philip comes to faith and then immediately draws in a cynical and grumpy Nathaniel. It's the classic 'one shall tell another' model that most of us of a certain age were brought up on. Jesus himself demonstrates it with Nicodemus and the Samaritan woman in chapters 3 and 4. It's a good model.

In Acts chapter 2, on the other hand, we get the definitive picture of the classic *'individual preacher.'* It's the Day of Pentecost, the church is energized and Spirit-filled, and Peter preaches a dynamic message with stunning results; another good model.

But increasingly I find myself drawn to a model suggested at the beginning of Mark's Gospel.

Mark's was the first gospel, a book written specifically to instruct the infant church. While John wrote to provoke belief, Mark wrote to promote practice and values. His goal was simply to answer the question: what did Jesus do, and what should we as his followers be doing in response? So chapter 1 gives us a great introduction to what Jesus did and taught. Then chapter 2 builds on that with an introductory model for our response. In contrast to the models of the 'individual soul winner', and the 'individual preacher', this is a model of *'community outreach.'*

Let's look at the first dozen verses of that chapter.

A few days later, when Jesus again entered Capernaum, the people heard that he had come home. So many gathered that there was no room left, not even outside the door, and he preached the word to them. Some men came, bringing to him a paralytic, carried by four of them. Since they could not get him to Jesus because of the crowd, they made an opening in the roof above Jesus and, after digging through it, lowered the mat the paralysed man was lying on. When Jesus saw their faith, he said to the paralytic, 'Son, your sins are forgiven.'

Now some teachers of the law were sitting there, thinking to themselves, 'Why does this fellow talk like that? He's blaspheming! Who can forgive sins but God alone?'

Immediately Jesus knew in his spirit that this was what they were thinking in their hearts, and he said to them, 'Why are you thinking these things? Which is easier: to say to the paralytic, "Your sins are forgiven", or to say, "Get up, take your mat and walk"? But that you may know that the Son of Man has authority on earth to forgive sins...' He said to the paralytic, 'I tell you, get up, take your mat and go home.' He got up, took his mat and walked out in full view of them all. This amazed everyone and they praised God, saying, 'We have never seen anything like this!' (Mk. 2:1–12).

This can be broken down into three essential elements.

1. *An outreach priority*

There are two types of people here. The first type are simply there to be blessed by Jesus. They want to hear him teach, they want to see him in action, they want to be in his presence. They press, they flock, they crowd. But essentially they're there for themselves. They're *punters*. And there's nothing wrong with that.

But it's the second type of people that captivate our interest and create the impact. They're not *punters*, they're *people carriers*. They are there not primarily for their own benefit or blessing, but rather to bring someone else to Jesus. They're there to see someone else's needs met, not their own.

It's all a matter of priorities.

If culture is an expression of our priorities, an outworking of the things we value, then it is the leaders' job to set those priorities. Either leaders shape the culture or the culture will end up shaping them.

The outreach culture demonstrated by this group of 'people carriers' arose from a shared conviction, worked out in practical action, that there was nothing more important than bringing a needy person to Jesus. The paralysed man gives us a picture of thousands outside the church. Without the proactive intervention of a group of believers, they have no way and absolutely no hope of ever getting to Jesus.

A while ago I spent a day with the leadership team of a particular church. I asked them to explain to me how they used their mid-week small group meetings in outreach. 'Actually', came the response, 'we see our home groups as a safe place for church members to have their own needs met. There's so much outreach activity in the rest of church life that we felt the need to create havens where it's just about us and Jesus.'

Now I have to be careful here, but I have a problem with that.

The overriding priority in Jesus' life was to 'seek and to save what was lost' (Lk. 19:10). He refused to create no-go areas for the seeker, but 'welcomed sinners' at every turn. When Jesus lost his cousin John, he withdrew privately with his disciples to a solitary place. They went to retreat, to mourn, and to recuperate after a time of extended outreach (Mt. 14; Mk. 6 and Lk. 9). But a crowd of lost people turned up anyway. Guess what: Jesus dropped everything and reached out to them. He even took on the catering. Why? Because it was his *priority*. That was the culture that he created for himself and his disciples. And it has to be ours, too.

The fact of the matter is that there are many people out there who will only come to faith in the context of a small group. The big, public meeting won't do it for them. The organized programme won't meet their need. But a small-scale community of outward-looking believers just might carry them to Jesus.

I'm not saying that we have to swamp the entire programme with outreach activities, running ourselves ragged at the expense of pastoral care, discipleship and teaching. But I *am* saying that leaders have to allow outreach to happen at every single level of church. We have to create access points at every conceivable level of church life; all possible doors have to be flung open. Compartmentalizing outreach simply does not work. As has often been said, 'It's not about putting outreach on the agenda. Outreach *is* the agenda.'.

In creating a culture of outreach, leaders have to prioritize mission. It has to be the number one goal in their own life and ministry. After all, you cannot lead what you do not live. Outreach has to be prioritized, profiled and modelled. The vision statement of the church has to reflect the values of the great commission. We have to praise good practice, and propagate good models. The budget has to underwrite it; the prayer strategy has to underpin it; worship and teaching have to underline it.

Of course, the irony is that the 'people carriers', just like the disciples at the feeding of the five thousand, end up being the ones most intimately and profoundly touched by the presence of Jesus.

2. *An outreach plan*

Establishing the right priorities is a good start, but it won't stop you from getting stuck.

This group of 'people carriers' quickly comes up against the same thing that every outreach activity comes up against. Obstacles. Make no mistake, the moment that you determine to reach out, to bring needy people to Jesus, you *will* hit difficulties. It applies to individuals, it applies to churches, and it applies here.

Mark tells us that although this group set out with the right priorities and the best of motives, they soon came to a place where they literally could go no further. They couldn't physically get the paralysed man to Jesus 'because of the crowd.'

Vision is not enough.

I've seen so many individuals set off bursting with passion and faith to reach their non-believing friends and family, only to wind up defeated, discouraged and derailed. I've seen it with churches, too. Programmes sputter out, initiatives get quietly dropped. We tried it, they say, and it didn't work.

The reality is, of course, that if you pursue a maintenance agenda things will tick along nicely; but opt for outreach and you'll quickly find yourself with a fight on your hands. Be it peer pressure, prevailing social attitudes, lifestyle choices, spiritual oppression or just plain old sin, you're going to hit roadblocks. The world, the flesh and the devil still conspire to stop people being brought to Jesus.

This is where evangelistic leadership comes into its own. For with every obstacle, there's an opening. All it takes is a plan.

The obstruction these friends encountered didn't deter them. Someone in the group came up with a plan, an idea of mad genius. It wasn't so much lateral thinking as vertical thinking. If we can't go through the crowd, they thought, we'll go over it. And so they create an opening in the roof of the house. It seems almost obvious now, we know the story so well. But at the time it was anything but.

Many churches fall down in outreach simply because they lack an effective plan. Creating a culture of outreach is about more than just sorting out priorities and trumpeting vision. Leaders have to know how to think strategically; how to overcome the obstacles, steer clear of the weaknesses, and anticipate the problems. In short, how to get effectively from A to B.

Too often we reach for the off-the-shelf solution, without working out a joined-up plan that considers the needs of our communities, the gifts of our people and the implications of our strategies. We need to be clear about the way forward, to engage the right people in the right things, to think through each stage in the process. We'll look more closely at some of these issues as we go through the book.

I was with a leadership team a few months ago, discussing their evangelistic strategy up to that point. One of the leaders put it this way: It's as if we've taken a bunch of stepping stones and just thrown them randomly into the river. It's difficult getting from one stone to the other, and our stones only take you as far as the middle of the river. We're good at meeting our community where they are; but we don't have an easy way for them to move forward to where we are or to come to faith.

The good news is that most churches don't need to do anything new to be effective. It's not unusual to find that all the key elements, giftings and programmes are there already. It's not a matter of discovering some new method. It's more about being strategic and effective with what you've already got. It's about structuring your thinking and marshalling your resources for mission. It's about devising simple steps and a game plan that everyone can understand and buy in to. It's about energizing the body, identifying goals, and providing simple, flexible, joined-up structures for growth. We'll unpack this all in greater detail in our final chapter.

3. An outreach people

But of course, the main thrust of this passage is not simply vision and strategy, priorities and plans. It's about man-power. This is a story about the potential of people and the power of a group committed to a common cause.

How do you picture this scene? Do you visualize four men and a stretcher, one on each corner? For most of my Christian life that's how I imagined it. Read the accounts in Matthew and Luke and you could be forgiven for making that very mistake. But Mark gives us the clearer insight. He tells us that: 'some men came, bringing to him a paralytic, carried by four *of them*' [italics added].

So this was a larger group than just four men. At any one time, four were in charge of carrying the man, but the total group could have been ten, twenty, fifty. They may have been neighbours from a particular street or the workforce of a business. We don't know how many there were, but it doesn't take more than a cursory glance to recognize that this was a labour intensive project.

You can imagine some servant-hearted types carrying the man on his mat; a creative visionary leader gets the idea to go for the roof; someone else breaks the plan into its logistical components, working out what they're going to need to break through the pitch, mortar, stone slabs and plaster of the roof, and then lower him down safely; (or did you think that they just *happened* to have shovels, picks, hammers and rope on them?) Some head back with a list of tools and where to find them; others stay to comfort and encourage the paralytic; some handle the refreshments, someone oversees the demolition, others motivate, everyone mans the ropes. It's a group triumph.

I recently met someone who used to work with the Mountain Rescue teams. He told me that when they got the call to go out, they would never leave with less than eighteen people. They would have six people to carry the stretcher at any one time, and then rotate that team with two other teams of six. He said it's hard work carrying someone to safety, so one person didn't do any carrying at all. Their job was simply to motivate the teams and keep everyone's spirits up.

Now *that's* a culture of outreach: everyone in the team focused on a common goal, able to play their part in seeking and saving a lost climber.

I'm inspired and impressed when I hear of one gifted Christian leading eighteen people to Christ. But I'm even more profoundly moved when I hear of eighteen ordinary Christians coming together to bring just one person to Christ. I believe that should be every church leader's normative model for outreach.

Cutting small corners

Ultimately in this incident salvation, forgiveness and healing are released because of faith. But it's not the faith of the paralysed man. He doesn't seem to do or say anything at all. He just walks out. That's his whole contribution to the story. Rather, it was when Jesus 'saw *their* faith, he said to the paralytic, "Son, your sins are forgiven".'

It's the faith of his *friends* that brings this individual to the forgiveness of Christ, incidentally also triggering this first, profound claim of divinity. Somehow we have to recapture the power of the united church community in outreach.

As a child, Sunday school taught me that I must let my little light shine. I had to be a candle, in my small corner. Somewhere else out there, in the gloomy darkness, other candles were in their small corners. Well, in the words of the game show host: it's good, but it's not right!

In Matthew 5, Jesus called his followers the 'light of the world.' He didn't tell them to aspire to or strive for it. He said they *were* it: 'You *are* the light of the world' (Mt. 5:14–16). But the powerful thing here is that he was speaking *corporately*, not individually. He didn't put the emphasis on each of them being individual lights. Rather, he said 'you' (plural) are the 'light' (singular) of the world.[2] As a community of faith, we are a city on a hill, not merely a few flickering candles. We are the lamp that, given the proper profile and visibility, gives light to the whole house.

How have we missed this? Frankly, I don't want to be in a small corner. It's way too lonely and ineffectual. I want to be in the middle of the room, at the top of the hill, on a huge stand with the rest of my brothers and sisters, part of an attractive, highly visible community of people-carriers.

Jesus said it was by our love that people would know we were authentic followers of Christ (Jn. 13:35). He prayed that we would be unified, so that the world would believe he was from God (Jn. 17:23). He told us to let our good

---

[2] The Greek word Jesus used for 'you' is in the plural, the collective form. Most English translations don't pick this up.

deeds be seen by the outside world, so that people would
end up giving glory to God.

We'll look closer at the dynamics of Christian community and its role in effective outreach in the second half
of the book. But for now, it's worth reminding ourselves
of the strong corporate, community emphasis of biblical
outreach. It's a natural, relational, releasing model.

Defining a culture of outreach

Exactly what is a culture of outreach, and what is it made
up of?

If we use the Mark 2 passage as our template then an
outreach culture is about outreach priorities, outreach plans
and outreach people. It's about heart, head and hands.

'Heart' is to do with the outreach priority and our
vision.

A culture of outreach is one where reaching lost people
and bringing them to Jesus is a priority in people's lives
and thinking, from the ordinary member to the senior
leader. Outreach is specifically woven into the vision of the
church, and informs every initiative, ministry and aspect
of church life. Outreach is an unconscious value for every
member of the community. Members are there not simply
for their own blessing, but in order to be people-carriers
for the lost, the last and the least.

'Head' is to do with the outreach plans and our
strategy.

A culture of outreach requires a thought through game
plan for touching society and winning people, one that is
simple enough for everyone to understand and buy in to,
yet involved enough to deal with all the challenges and
obstacles that inevitably crop up. A church's outreach plan
may be like a skeleton – well thought through, pervasive

and strategically connected, yet organic, flexible and hidden beneath the surface. For most members it may well be taken for granted, 'the way we do things round here.' Yet for leaders it is specific, detailed and constantly reviewed.

'Hands' is to do with the outreach people and our empowerment.

A culture of outreach is one where people are trained, equipped, envisioned and resourced to bring others to Jesus. It's about equipping every member as a missionary, yet at the same time unlocking the vast potential of the attractive community, enabling and stimulating corporate outreach. The emphasis is on releasing people, rather than relying on programmes. It's about allowing members to find success and fruitfulness in ways that flow with their individual gifts, personalities and experience, rather than shoe-horning them into an uncomfortable evangelistic stereotype.

A few years ago I had a conversation with Mary, a leader in a church that had struggled to stay afloat, never mind see conversion growth. She bemoaned the fact that she couldn't think of any real non-believing friends. 'I give myself so fully to the church,' she said. 'There's not really time to relate outside it.'

It's an all too familiar story, but as we talked things through she remembered a friend at work, and clutched on to that relationship as her one significant friendship outside church. She began praying for that woman. At the time I was there to provide training for church members, as well as working with the leaders to provide frameworks and strategy for outreach. Over a period of months it was exciting to see a culture steadily growing of valuing non-believing friends, praying for them together and looking for simple, natural ways of drawing them into the church community.

The next Alpha course the church ran was explosive. Instead of the one or two guests that they were used to getting, they now had over twenty. Mary's friend and her husband were part of that, and four months later they'd both come to faith. I love it when leaders' friends come to faith!

The best thing that happened to that church was that outreach got turned on its head. Before, they used to start with *programmes* like a guest service or an Alpha course, and then they'd ask the question: we have an initiative, who can we invite to it? Now they were starting with *people*, with their non-believing friends. They were building stronger relationships with them, praying for them, reaching out to them. Now the question was much more healthy: we have close non-believing friends, what can we invite them to?

I've watched that church almost double in size over a six-year period. They've outgrown two different venues in that time, and have now become one of the most evangelistically fruitful and influential churches in the area. They've developed an outreach culture that takes vision, strategy and empowerment seriously, and it has become embedded in the psyche of the entire church.

A culture of outreach is about people and process, not programmes and professionals. It's about starting with people that don't know Christ, and then reaching out to them in loving and appropriate ways, praying and seeing the power of God affecting their hearts, leading them through a natural process of discovering Jesus for themselves.

Then it's about the church programme becoming varied, flexible and appropriate to different needs, all to serve the organic outreach that is already taking place.

When you have a culture of outreach you should start expecting the unexpected. People will take the initiative in creative and unforeseen ways. They'll go 'off road' to win people to Jesus. They'll do things that nobody's done before or even thought of. It will happen naturally.

You better get used to the sound of digging overhead.

Everyone's too busy

It seems to me that one of the most common complaints among church leaders today is that everyone's too busy. Many leaders shy away from missional initiatives because their people are overloaded. We'd love to do this, they say, but we don't have the manpower. The same, keen people get asked to do the same key tasks. People lead busy, stressful lives; they get overcommitted quickly.

Some of you reading this will no doubt think what we are saying is appealing in theory, but fear the implications of yet more activity, more initiatives, more energy. You recognize that community outreach, outward focused groups, require leadership, and all your existing leaders are in danger of buckling under the weight they're carrying already. How do we move forward?

This is a crucial question. Vision and strategy are absolutely vital but, in and of themselves, they are not sufficient to produce an effective culture of outreach. There has to be a mobilizing of people, a harnessing of community life. And this is why I love Mark's account. For something like this to happen *someone* has to provide a lead. Someone has to take the initiative, maintain the motivation, devise a plan. Yet nobody in this story stands out. We don't even know their names. Leadership is there, but it's grass roots, empowering organic.

This is a key point to understand. A culture of outreach requires leadership, but that leadership becomes most effective when it is scattered *throughout* the church, as well as provided by those in positions of responsibility *over* the church. You need people at ground level, at the grass roots, who can provide a lead and exert positive influence. These 'grass roots evangelistic leaders' are vital in helping drive an outreach culture. Their attitude, their energy, their ideas, their encouragement, their initiative and their influence are the key to ensuring that a culture of outreach isn't simply a 'top down' directive, but a growing 'grass roots' movement.

If you've wrestled with the issue of people being too busy then this is good news for two reasons.

First of all, the reality is that there are already individuals in your church who have within themselves the potential and the desire to provide grass roots evangelistic leadership within the church. They hold the key to unlocking the potential for natural, lifestyle, relational outreach – particularly at the small group level. But because they don't tend to fit the usual pastoral profile, there is a good chance that they are not already committed to the hilt.

Often, members with this potential struggle to find a place of effectiveness and service in traditional church structures. Most of them will jump at the opportunity to express their gifts, exercise their passion and exert their influence. Paradoxically, building a culture of outreach can actually *release* an untapped work force, rather than loading more work on the usual suspects.

Secondly, though, grass roots evangelistic leadership requires investment, training, resources and development, no matter who you choose. There's a difference between having potential, and being equipped to fulfil a specific, strategic role. If we're going to see effective leadership at grass roots, then we need to train, mentor and teach for it. Too often the tendency is to *recruit* people to a job that needs doing, instead of *releasing* them to express their God-given gifts.

I've discovered that when we offer people development and investment opportunities, that merge and mesh with the vision and passion they already have, then it's a lot easier to gain their involvement. Suddenly, people aren't too busy after all.

In the next few chapters we'll look at how to develop grass roots evangelistic leadership in the church, how to mobilize every member for mission, and how to effectively shape culture. In Part 2, we'll discover how to make sure the core, prevailing conditions in church life are healthy enough for natural growth to take place. By the end of the book we'll look at some simple keys to help you structure and strategically plan for effective, intelligent outreach.

But for now, let's finish by summarizing the basic requirements for a culture of outreach:

1. *Outreach priority (vision)*

   - Leaders have to prioritize outreach in their own lives. They have to model it and live it, leading by example.

   - Leaders have to set outreach and disciple-making as the priority for church life. The vision statement, the communication, the budget, the prayer meeting and the programme have to reflect mission values.

   - Leaders have to make sure that an outward focus runs through every part of church culture and that access points for non-believers exist at every level of church life.

2. *Outreach plan (strategy)*

   - Leaders need to understand the principles of effective outreach and how people come to faith, and how to impact a community.

- Leaders need to understand and discern the obstacles that hinder outreach, and to find creative ways through them.

- Leaders need to understand the nature and strengths of their own church, and how to utilize these for outreach.

- Leaders need to be able to devise a strategic plan for outreach. They need to programme it, communicate it, oversee it and evaluate it.

- Leaders need to make sure that each member is engaged according to their strengths and motivations. They need to make sure that everyone understands the basic game plan and the part they have to play within it.

3. *Outreach people (empowerment)*

- Leaders have to identify individuals with the potential and gifting to deliver evangelistic leadership at grass roots. They have to train, engage, oversee and resource them.

- Leaders have to mobilize every member as a missionary, equipping, supporting and resourcing them.

- Leaders have to facilitate visible, attractive communities of faith, a light for the world. They have to create church programmes that complement and support small group outreach activity.

Questions for Leaders

1. Priority

- To what extent do we as leaders model an outreach priority in our own lives?

- What proportion of our budget is given to outreach, both in terms of equipping and supporting our members, and also in terms of activities, communication and initiatives for those outside church?

- What would an outreach culture look like in our context? (Go on, dream a bit!)

2. Plan

- How thought-through and joined-up is our outreach strategy right now?

- Is our approach multifaceted or are we relying on a 'one size fits all' model?

- What are the major obstacles that prevent us from reaching our communities for Jesus?

3. People

- How well equipped and confident are our members to reach out and bring others to faith?

- How visible is our church community to the outside world? Are we a light on a stand or a light under a bowl?

- Which individuals in our church demonstrate a gift for evangelism, and how well are we doing in harnessing their abilities and attitude to influence others?

Chapter 3

Every Member a Missionary

'Every heart with Christ is a missionary; every heart
without Christ is a mission field.'

Count Nikolaus Ludwig von Zinzendorf[1]

Compassion.

It's one of those biblical words that contain so much
more than we first realize. There's a raw, visceral power
there that's mostly lost in translation. Worse still, it's often
translated as 'pity', a small-hearted, mealy-mouthed excuse
of a word.

Yet this word is a special word, a Christological word,
used just twelve times in Scripture, and only ever used *of*
Jesus or *by* Jesus. The original Greek word is *'splanchnizomai'*,
from the root *'splanchnon'*, which is where we get our word
'spleen'. It means, to put it indelicately, 'bowels.'

To the ancient Jewish mind everything was located
eighteen inches lower than to our sensibilities. You didn't
think with your mind, you thought with your *heart*. That

---

[1] Zinzendorf (1700–60) was leader and founder of the Moravian
community, which birthed one of history's most potent and
influential missionary movements. It was a significant contact with
Moravian missionaries that led to the conversion of John Wesley. A
24/7 prayer chain started in the grounds of Zinzendorf's estate was
to go on unbroken for a hundred years.

was where you made your decisions, that was your moral centre. And you didn't feel with your heart, you felt with your *gut*, your insides, your very core.

For them, emotion was quite literally visceral and gutsy. Think about it and it makes a kind of raw sense. When you feel strong emotion, your insides churn; fall in love and your appetite goes; get nervous and your stomach fills with butterflies; attempt something courageous and you're going to need, well, guts.

So come Valentines Day, the romantic first-century Jewish male would no doubt send his beloved a card sporting a picture of forty foot of long intestine. With an arrow through it. Or maybe the lucky girl would get a bowel-shaped box of chocolates. Not exactly the Hallmark moment.

So, a sentiment that's not sentimental, but compelling and honest and raw just the same. Our word 'splanch-nizomai' literally means a moving, a wrenching of the guts. It's the most powerful picture of the most powerful emotion you can imagine. It's the literal equivalent of a broken heart, utterly devastating and emotionally overwhelming. There's no greater passion than compassion.

Compassion and the harvest

When Jesus was moved with this gut-wrenching, visceral compassion he always responded with a miraculous act. Moved with compassion, he fed the four and the five thousand, gave sight to the blind men outside Jericho, delivered the demoniac boy, healed the Galilean leper, raised to life the Widow of Nain's dead son.

But there's one exception. Matthew 9

Jesus went through all the towns and villages, teaching in their synagogues, preaching the good news of the kingdom and healing every disease and sickness. When he saw the crowds, he had *compassion* on them, because they were harassed and helpless, like sheep without a shepherd. Then he said to his disciples, "The harvest is plentiful but the workers are few. Ask the Lord of the harvest, therefore, to send out workers into his harvest field" (Mt. 9:35–38 – italics added).

Here is compassion on a global scale. It's about the multitudes and the ultimate harvest. Yet Jesus doesn't immediately move in to act miraculously himself. Despite his perfect, comprehensive ability to preach, teach and heal, he has a different vision: workers in the harvest field. This time the compassion-driven miracle of Christ comes through the mission-driven body of Christ.

Harvest imagery doesn't work too well for us these days. We see harvest through twenty-first-century eyes, and we picture a guy in a combine harvester wearing a Walkman. But look through first-century eyes and you'd see a *community* at work. When the harvest ripened they'd call for the butcher, the baker, the candlestick maker. It was all hands on deck, the whole community involved – young and old together, strong farm workers centre stage, frail widows at the margins.

Harvest was about people. It was labour intensive, grunt work that anybody could do. You just needed the bodies. If you had lots of workers engaged, then you could reap fully; if you only had a few workers then some crops would be left unharvested and rotting. It was all a question of manpower.

It took me many years before I realized the simple truth of this passage. I always used to think that the need of the harvest was the super-reaper, the gifted ministry that would single-handedly bring in the sheaves. Yet Jesus, surrounded by his very own hand-picked, divinely-trained super team of disciples, didn't look to them as the answer. Rather, he saw them *facilitating* the answer.

Some of these apostles would become so empowered by the Spirit, that their very shadows would heal the sick. Yet all Jesus asked of them was simply to 'ask the Lord of the harvest to send out workers.' There's nothing wrong with the harvest. It's ripe. And there's nothing wrong with the harvest workers. They're out there, even if they're not being put to work. The issue is *engagement*. Workers have to be got into the harvest field. Evangelistic leaders, whether at the core of church or at the grass roots, recognize that it's their responsibility to pray and to facilitate the engagement of the whole community of faith into harvest work.

Leaders, you have a tremendous harvest out there that is ripe for reaping. But the size of your harvest will be directly proportional to your effectiveness in engaging workers in the harvest fields. Ordinary, regular members of your church have to be empowered and engaged. We dare not simply put together programmes and initiatives, hoping for volunteers to be *recruited*. Our highest calling, as leaders and ministers responding to the compassionate brokenness of Christ, has to be to pray and to lead so that an army of harvest workers can be *released*.

Biblical harvest boils down to manpower. It's labour intensive, it's incarnational, it's life on life. The more of your members you can equip, empower and engage in lifestyle outreach, the more growth you will see.

Every heart without Christ is a mission field. It's our job to make sure that every member is a missionary.

Master model

So how do we help workers engage with the harvest field? How do we make sure that every member is able to play their part, and fulfil their outreach potential?

God is the Lord of the harvest. Harvest is his priority, and he is the one that will direct, instruct and empower. He is the one that ultimately brings the growth. But what do *we* need to do as co-workers with Christ? What is the part that we have to play, if we want to be evangelistic leaders?

Here are four key steps to start with

1. Evangelistic leaders need to understand the fundamental biblical principles of outreach.

2. Evangelistic leaders need to make sure that every member is taught the principles of outreach, and is able to live them out effectively. Part of that teaching has to come from leaders modelling the example.

3. Evangelistic leaders need to design church programmes that support and facilitate members at each stage of lifestyle outreach.

4. Evangelistic leaders need to create structures that nurture and enable the process over the long haul, rather than just the short push.

In short, you have to know it, you have to teach it, you have to programme it and you have to structure it.

We'll look at some of the programme and structure issues later on in the book, but for now let's begin with the key *principles* of outreach.

In looking at these principles, it's helpful to consider that healthy, lifestyle outreach has both a discipleship aspect and a community aspect. We'll tackle the corporate, community aspect in Chapter 5, by looking at what Jesus *taught*. But first we need to start with outreach principles for the individual disciple, by looking at what Jesus *modelled*.

I believe there are three major keys for us here.

1. Jesus related to people where they were

When God set about winning back the human race, he didn't send a million gospel tracts fluttering down from the heavens. Rather, he became a person and related to other people where they were.

There is a place for mass communication, and the impersonality of print and broadcast media. But the best, most effective, most biblical outreach will always be primarily relational and incarnational.

Incarnation is the message, the good news, wrapped up in a body. Incarnation is all about *becoming* and *relating*. It's about points of contact, the overlap of life and experience. Jesus, the word made flesh, went to where people were and spoke their language. While every other teacher was telling parables about kings and governors and royal court intrigue, Jesus told simple stories about sheep and coins and seeds. He dealt with the ordinary experience of ordinary people. Jesus met with people and built bridges with them. He befriended them, ate with them and spent time with them. That's incarnation.

Effective outreach is so hugely labour intensive because it's all about life-on-life bridge building. Each of us can only invest significantly in a few key relationships at a time. That's why the best hope for the harvest is a mass mobilization of workers. If you want to have real impact, you have to have real contact.

Consider how much of Jesus' teaching and proclamation took place over the dinner table. In Luke 19 we find him interrupting the triumphal entry to eat with the 'sinner' Zacchaeus. Repentance, restitution and salvation result. In Matthew 9 we see Jesus partying with a motley crew of tax collectors: thugs and scoundrels so morally bankrupt that their sworn testimony was not valid in a court of law. When criticized, Jesus replied that this was how he fulfilled his mission of calling sinners. In Luke 7 Jesus proves himself an equal opportunity diner, eating and teaching in the home of Simon the Pharisee.

The list goes on and on: the wedding feast of Cana (Jn. 2), the home of Mary and Martha (Lk. 10), not to mention the miraculous feedings of the crowds. What a huge battery of theology and doctrine is contained in John 13 – 16. Yet all of it occurs in the context of a Supper. When I read about Jesus giving his disciples the new command to love, I picture him talking, mouth half full, breadcrumbs in his beard.

In Luke 15 Jesus tells the world's most famous parable, the story of the lost son. Yet the chapter starts by informing us that Jesus 'welcomed sinners and ate with them.' It wasn't just that he went into their homes; he also invited them to be where he was. He *welcomed* them. That's how he earned the nickname 'friend of sinners.' It was a derogatory term, a criticism of his character and his morality. It was guilt by association, and it went hand in hand with the other Pharisaic slur he picked up, 'glutton and drunkard' (Lk. 7:34).

Yet it is instructive to us as Christ-followers. Jesus-style outreach takes place in the context of friendship and bridge building. It happens in the natural rhythms of shared life – over the dinner table, at the party, in the outdoors. It's about invitation and identification.

(a) Pros and cons

Our first foundational principle for lifestyle outreach is therefore this

People bring people – relationships are the key

Relational outreach is essentially building bridges from one heart to another, so that Jesus can walk across. Studies have shown that we will usually be most effective at reaching out to people that are like us. That's because we're usually able to build the strongest relationships with those with whom we share similar interests, background, personality type or stage of life.

A few years ago a survey was conducted, asking people what first brought them to church.

- 1 per cent came through cold contact door-to-door outreach

- 2 per cent came because of a special programme put on by the church

- 3 per cent came because of Sunday school

- 3 per cent came because of a personal crisis or problem

- 6 per cent came because of publicity

- 8 per cent came because of contact with the minister

- 77 per cent came because of a friend or a relative

Now we need to make sure that we cover all the bases. Some people will never come to faith without cold contact, pioneer outreach; others will come purely because of our publications, our advertising, our social programmes. But the absolute vast majority will come through relationships.

The sad reality is that most Christians are at their most effective in outreach during their first year as believers. After that time their connections, their relationships and their relevance to those outside the church drops off significantly. Keeping or regaining that initial sharpness can be difficult.

For most Christians there are three 'cons' associated with relational outreach. Either there's no *con*tact, where

Christians live in a 'spiritual apartheid' ghetto, with no real significant relationships with non-believers. Or there's no *con*trast, where Christians have plenty of good friendships with non-believers, but they identify to the point of being identical. There's simply no distinctiveness about them that would build bridges and draw others to Christ.

Finally, there's no *con*sistency, where Christians find themselves living two separate lives depending on the context, having one set of behaviours for church, another for the rest of life. It's a schizophrenic lifestyle, a kind of 'Dr Jekyll, Mr Christian' dualism.

The challenge is to encourage and equip our members for real engagement with the world. We have to teach them how to develop stronger relationships and with whom. We have to model the example, with every leader giving themselves to significant non-church friendships. And we have to create the culture where an outward-looking, loving, missionary mindset is the absolute norm.

Jesus related to people where they were. But then what?

2. *Jesus loved people and met their needs*
One of the most striking questions that Jesus ever asked people was this: 'What do you want me to do for you?'

It's one of those classic Jesus questions that crops up consistently in his interactions, and it totally wrongfoots our perceptions of evangelism. To start with, we're so used to presenting answers that asking questions has become almost alien to us. And then for Jesus to allow the 'sinner' to set the agenda seems perverse. After all, *he's* the Saviour, we should be asking what we can do for *him*. To make things worse, people almost invariably give the wrong answer. The blind men ask for sight, the leper asks for healing. Nobody ever asks for forgiveness of sins, or to follow him.

Yet here's the surprise. Jesus gives them what they want. He meets the basic, superficial needs that they feel. Then the real miracle happens, they take the next step themselves. They follow him.

Jesus loved people enough to serve them. He found out the needs that they had, the needs that seemed most pressing and he met them. Sometimes Jesus showed acute perception, seeing past appearances and discerning the most fundamental need. We get that with our Mark 2 paralysed man, when his first act is to forgive the man's sins. Healing comes almost as a bonus, to help illustrate a point. But the fundamental need revolves around crippling guilt and Jesus goes straight to it.

This meeting of needs wasn't just a personal style for Jesus, but a command for all wanting to follow him. When asked the question, 'How do I inherit eternal life?' Jesus told the story of the Good Samaritan. Read it again in Luke 10 and you'll see a consummate example of meeting needs: emotional, physical, medical and financial. Incidentally, the first need met was for an emotional connection. It was about love. The Samaritan was moved with compassion. And, yes, it *is* that very word that we started with: the only time that extraordinary gut wrenching emotion is used of an ordinary human being. And it's in the context of a 'go and do likewise' command.

(a) Slavery, the secret to success

Without compromising on the message, and without dropping the difficult narrow-gate demands of discipleship, Jesus was able to open people up to higher possibilities by meeting the needs that they actually felt.

This then gives us our second foundational principle

Love people by meeting the needs they feel

It's a psychological truth that people only care about the needs they feel. If you're lonely then you want a friend: fulfilment can wait. If you're dying of thirst then you want water: ultimate meaning comes much lower down the list. That's why so many postpone issues of faith, earmarking them for old age. Right now, there are more than enough other needs to be getting on with.

A survey published by the Evangelical Alliance asked people what stopped them from coming to church

- 20 per cent said they didn't come because the message lacked relevance

- 33 per cent said they didn't come because the needs of their families came first

- 25 per cent said they didn't come because they thought church was boring

- 25 per cent said they didn't come because of those already there[2]

That's a stark indictment of our ability to meet the needs of those outside the church. Our messages don't relate to the needs and issues of ordinary people, and the pressing needs of families are threatened, not met, by church. Don't even get me started on those last two.

Too often the church offers answers to questions that people aren't asking. Offering to meet needs that people aren't aware of makes us at best an irrelevance, and at worse a nuisance. The problem doesn't lie with our answers, but with our timing. We have to learn to first address the needs that people actually *feel*.

There's an illuminating passage in 1 Corinthians 9 where Paul, that master missionary and soul winner, revealed the

---

[2] All figures rounded up.

secret to his success. What was it that made him so effective in bringing people to Jesus? Was it his insightful preaching, his sharp intellect, his powers of logical argument? Was it raw charisma, miraculous signs, a rare personal gift? Paul cited none of those, though he had them in abundance. Rather he said this: 'I make myself a slave to everyone, to win as many as possible' (1 Cor. 9:19).

Paul saw serving people, literally making himself their slave, as the most effective way to win as many as possible. That was his grand strategy for relational outreach. Again, it's an incarnational model, all about *becoming* and identifying. Paul goes on to list the ways in which he relates to different types of people. He *becomes* like a Jew to win the Jew, he *becomes* weak to win the weak, and so on. His secret is this: I have become all things to all men so that by all possible means I might save some (1 Cor. 9:22). Paul started where people were. Rather than looking for them to become like him, he became like them. The key to them believing is in us becoming.

How different our outreach would be if we started with the needs of those that we are trying to reach. Jesus, the perfect Servant, was humble enough to ask people what they wanted, as well as asking the Father for direct insight. Not a bad strategy, that. That's why a community survey can be a great starting-point for a church's outreach plan.

On a personal level, it most often boils down to taking the time to get to know people, to ask questions, to find points of identification and becoming. The needs are usually basic – friendship, support, a listening ear, practical help, community, belonging and acceptance. All needs that we, as followers of Christ, are well placed to meet. This is not beyond our reach. This is something that any one of us can do.

The motivation to love and serve must come with no strings attached. Yet the almost inevitable consequence is that, as initial felt needs are met and sorted, the deeper spiritual needs, fundamental to every human being, rise to prominence. The good news becomes relevant.

So far, so nice and safe. But where's the cutting edge?

3. *Jesus touched people with God's power*

Take even the most cursory glance at the outreach of Jesus and you find yourself overwhelmed by the presence of the miraculous.

Jesus brought the power of God to bear on so many of his interactions with people. He related to people where they were, he built bridges with them, he understood them and served them, but he also connected them with the power of God. He healed them, he delivered them, he changed them through supernatural insight and knowledge.

Many people dismiss relational outreach as an easy, touchy-feely option. For some, so-called 'friendship evangelism' is a cop-out. All friendship, no evangelism. So it's important to see that Jesus-style outreach is relational and natural, and yet at the same time dynamic and supernatural.

This gives us our third principle:

Only the power of God can change hearts

Ultimately salvation is a divine, supernatural transaction, and the most basic way this works out in our outreach is through prayer. Prayer brings the supernatural power of God to bear on a person's life. There's no salvation without prayer being there somewhere in the mix.

The foundational parable for outreach is the Parable of the Sower. Here we see the phases of outreach that we're used to – sowing and reaping. Yet the parable is about much more than that. It's basically a study of what you sow into, what condition a person's heart must be in for God's word to be fruitful in their lives. It's not so much about sowing techniques or the art of reaping, but rather about the soil that you start with.

Jesus related different soil types to different heart conditions. The soil on the path is hardened and down-trodden, the thorny soil is choked with worries, cares and materialism, the stony soil is shallow and superficial. And none of them will ever produce a crop unless something fundamental changes.

If our outreach is limited to sowing and reaping we will remain fruitless most of the time. We need to begin with groundwork. The ground has to be prepared, the soil made good.

That's why the incarnational approach is so vital. It's as we touch lives, build bridges, meet needs that we prepare hearts to receive the message. Yet clearly some heart issues – hardness, shallowness, the deceitfulness of wealth, a lack of revelation – can only be tackled through prayer and the power of God.

(a) Preparing the way

Most Christians have no clear idea of how to pray effectively for their non-believing friends. So many go no further than praying variations on 'Dear God, let my friend become a Christian!' That's all well and good as a starting-point, but try praying that consistently for more than a couple of weeks and you'll see it getting old very fast. So how do you pray for non-believing friends without getting bored, and without boring God?

A key passage comes in Luke 3, where John the Baptist's mission is outlined. He came to prepare the way for the entrance of Christ, and his message was profound

Prepare the way for the Lord, make straight paths for him.
Every valley shall be filled in, every mountain and hill
    made low.
The crooked roads shall become straight, the rough ways
    smooth.
And all mankind will see God's salvation. (Lk. 3:4–6)

Anything that says, 'meet these conditions and God's salvation will result', merits further study. Here, when John talked about preparing the way by filling in valleys and levelling mountains, he was referring to a common practice when a town or village was preparing for the visit of a VIP.

The tradition then was not to roll out a red carpet, but rather to 'prepare the way.' A steward was sent on ahead to lead a work team. Their job was to move along the route the VIP would take, and remove every obstacle. In an area prone to mud and landslides, it was vital that stones and stumbling blocks be removed from the paths. If there were potholes they would be filled, if there were bumps in the road they would be levelled. The last thing you wanted was for your dignitary to be jolted out of their carriage, or brought to an undignified standstill because of some obstruction.

John's message was that Jesus was so far greater than any mere ruler, that it wasn't enough to clear away a few rocks and fill a few potholes. This was someone for whom you levelled entire mountains and filled whole valleys. Putting it simply, if you want to see the salvation of God, the entrance of Christ into a community or a single heart, you have to deal with the obstructions.

Effective prayer for the lost is about levelling mountains and filling valleys. It's about making the crooked paths straight and the rough ways smooth. It's understanding that people are in a place of paralysis where they cannot come to Christ. There are obstacles in their way – spiritual blindness, negative perceptions, peer pressure, ignorance, materialism, cultural issues, worries and cares. Effective prayer first of all seeks revelation of the obstacles and then sets about dealing with them one at a time.

Before we can hope to impact a person's heart fully with the gospel, there's usually a whole process of preparation that needs to be prayed through. Praying for someone to become a Christian is literally the last thing you should do.

(b) Mobilizing the missionaries

These then are our three basic principles

1. People bring people, relationships are the key.
2. Love people by meeting the needs they feel.
3. Only the power of God can change hearts.

As soon as we grasp these principles, our next responsibility as evangelistic leaders is to both model the principles ourselves and teach them to every member.

In our own work with churches, we created equipping and teaching resources, then piloted, developed and honed them over a period of about five years. The key with any training initiative is not simply to shove more cups of coffee into the fridge, but to work to fundamentally affect the culture of a church. As well as an initial 'kick start' course, we made sure that regular, relevant teaching was drip-fed into small group life by key individuals who'd grasped the vision and were being trained and mentored themselves.

It's not within the scope of this book to give a blow-by-blow rundown of an outreach equipping course. But if you'd like some more information on the resources that we've developed, then you can find an overview of that teaching and training in Appendix C.

However you go about teaching and building these principles, it's important to make sure that your equipping process answers these basic questions

1. How do we know who to reach out to?
2. How do we build bridges with people?
3. How can we play to our own strengths and find an outreach style that complements our personality? Is there an evangelism that works for the rest of us?
4. How do we identify with people and relate to them without compromise?
5. How do we reach out to people and build relationships when our lives are already so busy?
6. How do we discover what needs people actually feel, and how do we meet those needs?
7. How do we identify obstacles, and how do we pray effectively about them?
8. How do we share our stories and communicate our Christian experience naturally and creatively?
9. How can we understand and communicate the basics of the gospel? What are the most effective ways to 'sow truth' into a person's life?
10. How do we deal with difficult questions, and how do we help people move forward in their spiritual journeys?
11. How do we know when a person is ready to commit their lives to Christ, and how do we help them take that step?
12. How do we nurture and disciple new believers?

All this is just half the story. We've looked at the discipleship aspect of outreach, the individual missionary model.

But we also need to consider the community aspect. Outreach becomes most enjoyable and most potent when we engage in it *corporately* together. At its best, outreach is a team sport, as well as a full contact sport.

This is, for many, the missing ingredient and can revolutionize our experience. To get at these principles we need to move from what Jesus *modelled* as an individual, to what Jesus *taught* his followers as a community.

But before we move on, we need to look at a vital question – where exactly did the evangelist go in all of this?

Questions for Leaders

1. People bring people, relationships are the key

- How effective are we at empowering workers in the harvest? Do we concentrate more on importing 'super-reapers' than we do on facilitating a community of ordinary reapers?

- Can we identify the 'cons' working against members of our congregations? What can we do to help people overcome them?

2. Love people by meeting the needs they feel

Consider the EA survey, p. 46. How relevant are our messages to the world outside? How can our church reach families whose needs seem to clash with our programme? What about the issue of the church being boring? How can we lead our members so that they attract non-believers to church, rather than deterring them?

- Do we know what the felt needs are of the community we serve? How could we more effectively meet those needs?

3. *Only the power of God can change hearts*

- Do our members understand how to pray effectively and consistently for their non-believing friends? How can we make prayer for the lost creative and a natural part of our culture?

- How much does prayer for the lost, for the witnesses and for outreach feature in our united prayer meetings? How much is it built into our small group life?

Chapter 4

Evaluating the Evangelist

> 'My mother went into the Peace Corps when she was sixty-eight. My one sister is a motorcycle freak, my other sister is a holy roller Evangelist and my brother is running for president. I'm the only sane one in the family.'
>
> Billy Carter[1]

What is it about the evangelist and the church? Why is the relationship often such a mixed blessing? In the family of the church, the evangelist comes across as the visiting uncle, the loveable rogue; exciting, a little dangerous, often delightful – but mostly disconnected from the everyday realities of family life.

Evangelists are typically characterized as lacking in subtlety, driven by a narrow focus, seeing things in black and white. Speaking as an evangelist, I think there are a number of reasons for the cliché. The most compelling is probably the fact that we lack subtlety, are driven by a narrow focus, and see things in black and white.

I remember growing up in church and being exposed to visiting evangelists. They all seemed so much larger than

---

[1]   Billy Carter, brother of former US president Jimmy Carter.

life – big Bibles, big hair, big teeth, big stories. The best of those stories tended to take place on public transport, usually on airplanes for added glamour.

Typically the evangelist would get on a plane, headed off on yet another adventure. It was little surprise that the evangelist would immediately set to sharing their faith with the person sitting next to them. Wouldn't you know it – before the plane had even taken off that person had usually come to faith, weeping in the aisles?! Twenty minutes into the flight the new believer has shared their testimony with the other people in their row. They've all become Christians too, and are now having a prayer meeting for the rest of the plane.

By the time the flight comes into land, the entire planeload are singing *Shine, Jesus, Shine*. The hostesses are taking up an offering. The captain's leading a Bible study over the Tannoy. Even the plane itself has magically come to faith and is flapping its wings for joy …

That's an exaggeration. But it highlights the basic tension often found between church and evangelist. On the one hand, the evangelist is the bombastic motivator, a cheerleader for bold, faith-filled outreach; on the other, they often embody a model that most people struggle to emulate. They can inspire and alienate the church in almost equal measure.

But make no mistake. The evangelist is a gift from Christ to his church. Unless that gift is properly utilized, unless the evangelist is engaged at the heart of church life, no church can grow and succeed as it should.

The questions is, how *do* we engage the evangelist? How does the gift best operate? And how do we help the church get the best out of the evangelist? Even more key, how do we help the evangelist get the best out of the church?

Papering over the cracks

I started evangelistic ministry in the classic mould.
Working as a national evangelist for a para-church youth
organization, I travelled from church to church leading high
profile missions and outreach events. It was a good life.
They gave you a car and cool equipment. You got to drive
around, visit places and eat other people's food. And, yes,
you did have adventures; sometimes on public transport.

But equally there was frustration from the short-term
nature of so much church involvement. After a while you
began to feel like some spiritual painter/decorator. You
were brought in to do a job that people didn't feel confident
doing themselves. They hoped that you could make things
look better without costing too much or making too much
mess. And if you could do that while they were away on
holiday then so much the better!

Again, it's an exaggeration. But that's what it felt like.
Going back to visit churches a few months down the line
was almost invariably discouraging. Yes, some of the
results had stuck, but very rarely did you see significant,
lasting change and growth. It's simply naïve to think that
you can get long-term results from short term measures.

After a number of years I switched gears into local
church leadership, looking to see how the evangelistic
gifts might fit more holistically into church life, rather
than simply being bolted on from time to time.

It seemed to me that people with an evangelistic gift
could end up in one of three different positions in church:
above the church, at the edge of the church, or under the
church.

1. *Above the church*
This is a classic route for people with strong evangelistic
gifting. It means that you operate almost outside of

the regular church structures. You go and join a para-church set up, a mission organization, a team of outreach specialists.

It's easy to see why. Church leadership classically tends to be dominated by those whose main gifting is weighted towards the pastoral. That poses two main problems for the evangelist.

First of all, it's difficult to see how they fit in. Small group leadership usually falls to the pastorally hearted, as does senior leadership. The clash between the pastorally motivated and the evangelistically motivated is well established. It comes back down to that focused, forceful mentality; the impatient evangelist in the grip of a strong, black and white vision. Too often they rub against the more considered, touchy-feely, caring pastor looking at the big picture, waiting till conditions are just right. Beyond the clichés and the generalizations, though, there's real potential for friction. The evangelistically gifted can be a thorn in the flesh of the more pastorally minded, whilst at the same time feeling misunderstood, stifled and frustrated.

The second issue is more pragmatic. If you have a strong evangelistic gift and calling, where do you go to get that developed? Where can you be shaped, honed and mentored? Where are the models for you to follow, the opportunities for you to pursue, the chances for you to shine? Rarely is this in local church. You have to look outside. Birds of a feather do tend to flock together, and often they flock to para-church set ups. Sometimes they flock further afield to other mission opportunities.

Perhaps the clearest example of the evangelist existing 'above' the church is the crusade evangelist, a renowned and recognized ministry that operates on a different level all together to local church. Usually the church buys in to this ministry, often coming under a wider initiative that spans a number of churches. It's high impact, high profile, high altitude.

It's above the church.

This is not a criticism of the crusade model or of para-church initiatives. These are vital and powerful ministries that the church would be all the poorer without. I owe an enormous and profound debt to ministries such as these. They have served the church well, and left an indelible mark on my life and the lives of many thousands of others.

But the question remains, is this the closest the evangelist gets to the heart of church? Do they operate best as free-spirited service providers? Can they only ever be truly fulfilled away from the grass roots?

2. *At the edge of church*

It seems to me that in so many churches the place that you'll find people with evangelistic gifting is towards the edges.

Church growth theorists estimate that with any given congregation, somewhere between 5 and 10 per cent have a level of evangelistic gifting. They may not conform to some clichéd mould, they may vary in approach, temperament and charisma. But they do share a passion for those outside the church, a natural motivation to reach out, an ease in connecting beyond the four walls of church. They have a gift for evangelism. And that gift needs to be outworked.

You'll find them in the youth group or working the youth club; you'll find them involved with prison ministry and hospital visitation; you'll see them working in schools outreach or on the streets; you'll encounter them working with the elderly, helping with Mums and Tots, running Alpha courses, leading workplace evangelism. They have enormous energy, drive and enthusiasm, and it's all directed outside the church. It's located at the edges, on the margins, at the borders.

Now this makes perfect sense. If your gift is in outreach, and your motivation is for outreach, then you want to be where the church most tangibly reaches out and touches the world. But there's a problem. It's called the 'Doughnut Church'.

The doughnut church is like a ring doughnut where all the lip-smacking good stuff is at the edge. But in the middle there's just a void, emptiness. Essentially you have a minority of people engaged in outreach at the edges, while the vast majority of church remain unfruitful, unproductive and unengaged. According to Barna research, 95 per cent of Christians have never led anyone else through to faith in Christ. It's doughnut church syndrome. Good activity on the borders, almost nothing to speak of at the heart.

It gets worse. With people of clear gifting and commitment doing so well on the edges, the temptation is for the rest of the church to feel validated by their efforts. 'We're not being particularly fruitful as a home group', they'll say. 'But we're okay, because plenty is happening with the young people, or in the schools.' And so the commission for each follower of Christ to be a witness, to bear fruit, is abdicated.

More desperate still, those reached by the various initiatives find it fundamentally difficult to find their way into church. The prevailing culture is not one of outreach and inclusion, but self-preservation and inertia. People won on the margins of mainstream church life and consciousness often end up staying there. The fact is, churches with good activities on the edges don't necessarily grow. Something much more fundamental needs to happen at the heart.

3. *Under the church*

At the risk of morbidity, the church has a history of burying evangelists. Some don't operate above the church or at the edge of the church, they end up underneath the church.

The problem with the evangelistically motivated is that they often have little patience for the humdrum, day-to-day business of church. They have big hearts and big dreams. They don't care what songs get sung, how the room gets set out, what the teaching programme is. They want to be out there winning the world. They're passionate, visionary and focused. The problem is, they're often a lot more fragile than people realize. Insecurity is almost part of the job description. It's easy for them to become discouraged and disillusioned with church.

A number of years ago, I spent time with a church leadership team and talked about the way they engaged their evangelistically gifted members. I spoke about evangelists 'over, at the edge and under', and when I was finished the senior leader responded. 'We're pretty good here,' he said. 'I don't think any of our evangelistic people feel like that.'

He turned for a confirmation to a female colleague with a strong evangelistic gift. She promptly burst into tears. 'I've felt all three of those things at different times,' she said. 'People think I'm thick skinned, but I'm really not. I struggle to know how to fit in and be myself. I feel deeply for the lost. When people joke about me being over the top, it hurts. I feel pain for the world, and I feel rejection from the church.'

It's not always easy when your main gifting and motivation is in reaching out to people outside the church. A recent survey reported by the Evangelical Alliance revealed that 40 per cent of people in the UK believe it is wrong for Christians to share their beliefs with others. Some of that hostility and antipathy to faith sharing exists even within the church. So many with evangelistic gifting have felt badly treated and burnt.

Of course, sometimes evangelists are their own worst enemies.

I remember speaking to a particularly fiery young man once when I was part of the leadership team of a large and influential church. I shared with him my goals for outreach, my vision for the year, the number of people we wanted to see brought to faith in the next twelve months. I made a play for him to get involved, to knuckle down, to help us make the goal a reality. He did everything but spit on my shoes.

'Is that all?' he said. 'I could see that number of people come to faith on my own.' He was the leadership's worst nightmare. Every bit the bull horn wielding, fire and brimstone preaching, in your face, loose cannon stereotype; a real pain in the home group.

He quickly ended up discouraged and disillusioned, and six months later he'd dropped out of church life. That was the way it went with him every couple of years. I've seen so many gifted evangelistic people end up that way. So many colleagues over the years have ended up losing their respect for church, so many have become cynical and embittered. Some have lost faith altogether.

It's not always so dramatic. Some don't drop out, but rather quietly and gradually give up. They stay around, but the fire begins to die within them. They're still in church, still have faith, but they give up, shut down and sputter out.

Somehow the church has to do better in harnessing the evangelistic gift and ministry. Without it, long term, vital growth is just not possible for a church. It's a fundamental health issue.

The church needs the evangelist.

Looking to Scripture

But what exactly does a healthy evangelistic ministry look like? What is the precise role of the evangelist in local church? How is the evangelist supposed to fit into everyday church life?

It makes sense to look to Scripture for answers. Interestingly enough, the word 'evangelist' is recognized and used in Scripture – unlike the word 'evangelism.'

'Evangelism' is a modern addition that all too often confuses the issue. It compartmentalizes the concept of outreach, pigeon-holing it away from mainstream discipleship. It sends out the signal that reaching the world is the province of the evangelist. Evangelism for the evangelist. Outreach becomes an optional extra for those that way inclined; an 'add on' for the young and the reckless.

'Evangelist', however, *is* a biblical term, coming from a Greek word for 'herald of good news.' The picture is of a messenger sent back from a battlefield to relay news of military victory. The *euangelistes* proclaimed a message of deliverance, salvation and peace to a jubilant populace. These were the guys with 'blessed feet', running back to the city at full tilt, a sight for sore eyes.

We find the term 'evangelist' used only three times in the New Testament, but each time is instructive. Each builds upon our basic concept of 'herald of good news' to reveal a rounded and vital ministry.

1. *The empowering evangelist*

Let's look first at Ephesians 4, the roll call of ministry gifts.

> But to each one of us grace has been given as Christ apportioned it. This is why it says: 'When he ascended on high, he led captives in his train and gave gifts to men.' (What

does 'he ascended' mean except that he also descended to the lower, earthly regions? He who descended is the very one who ascended higher than all the heavens, in order to fill the whole universe.)

It was he who gave some to be apostles, some to be prophets, some to be evangelists, and some to be pastors and teachers, to prepare God's people for works of service, so that the body of Christ may be built up until we all reach unity in the faith and in the knowledge of the Son of God and become mature, attaining to the whole measure of the fullness of Christ.

Then we will no longer be infants, tossed back and forth by the waves, and blown here and there by every wind of teaching and by the cunning and craftiness of men in their deceitful scheming. Instead, speaking the truth in love, we will in all things grow up into him who is the Head, that is, Christ. From him the whole body, joined and held together by every supporting ligament, grows and builds itself up in love, as each part does its work (Eph. 4:7–16, italics added).

The ministry of the evangelist couldn't get a higher endorsement. It is a gift given to the church by none less than the risen Christ himself. The evangelists find they are in the company of apostles, prophets and pastor/teachers, as part of a dream team assembled to lead the church towards Christ-like maturity.

And yet look at the purpose for these gifts. Paul puts the emphasis firmly on *empowerment*. The gifts are there 'to prepare God's people for works of service.' Along with the other ministry gifts, the evangelist's main calling is the preparation of people for service.

Now the fact that such a ministry will have particular gifts and abilities to proclaim good news and lead others to faith is assumed. It's inherent in the very name, herald. Just as teachers will obviously teach, shepherds will shepherd, and prophets will prophesy, so 'proclaiming heralds' will clearly proclaim and herald.

But the key purpose for giving the gifts in the first place is focused not on the ministries themselves, but on the people that they prepare. Too often we see evangelists as gifted individuals who simply fulfil their own fantastic potential, while the people turn out to watch and applaud. Ephesians shows us that the genuine ministry is more about releasing God's people to fulfil *their* fantastic potential. The works of ministry (literally, service) are done by the people, not the professionals. The evangelist is just part of the support team, the coaches, the back room brigade.

And notice the result of effective evangelistic ministry; unity and maturity. Without the evangelistic ministry operating effectively in church, we can't reach true unity together. In a very pragmatic way, there is nothing more effective in bringing groups of believers together than a shared passion to proclaim good news. Nothing crosses borders of tradition, methodology and theology more potently.

Not only that, but the evangelist is part of the package given by Jesus to his church to bring each member to full *maturity*. They are indispensable for God's people to grow in discipleship, to mature in understanding and to flourish in relationship with Christ. The church can grow neither numerically, nor spiritually, without the input and intervention of the evangelist.

It's not just the world that needs the evangelistic gift. It's the church.

2. *The engaged evangelist*
Let's look next at Acts 21.

We continued our voyage from Tyre and landed at Ptolemais, where we greeted the brothers and stayed with

them for a day. Leaving the next day, we reached Caesarea
and stayed at the house of *Philip the evangelist*, one of the
Seven. He had four unmarried daughters who prophesied
(Acts 21:7–9, italics added).

This is a significant passage as it highlights the only person
in Scripture to be given the title 'evangelist.' Clearly, the
term 'evangelist' was not simply a theoretical ideal,
but a concrete, defined and recognized role. You could
point to Philip of Caesarea and see the role of evangelist
personified. And that's exactly what Luke does, writing
Acts. He points to Philip and pastes the label, 'evangelist',
to his forehead.

But there's a twist. He doesn't do it until chapter 21.

The interesting thing is that Philip pops up much earlier
in Acts, but without the big title. Luke reminds us that
this Philip was one of the seven, magnificently chosen in
Acts 6, not to be confused with Philip the Apostle, of the
original twelve.

Philip was cherry-picked from the entire population
of Jesus-followers to take administrative heat away from
the twelve apostles. The seven were judged to be men of
wisdom, filled with the Holy Spirit and wisdom, anointed
and commissioned to serve the church in practical ways.
Their first task was to administer the aid programme for
disadvantaged widows. Forget your so-called dichotomy
between social action and outreach. With the early church,
the poster boy for evangelism *was* the guy running the
social action.

And yet, in Acts 6, Philip is not called the evangelist.

When persecution sent the church splintering out-
wards, Philip goes to Samaria and proclaims the gospel
there with incredible results. An entire city in the region
is impacted. It's dramatic stuff. There are miraculous
healings, deliverance, baptisms. A city filled with joy. Later

on the apostolic leaders come in to deepen and build upon the work Philip has started. He's a team player.

To top it off, Philip is summoned by a real live angel for a desert rendezvous with a seeking Ethiopian official. After a master-class in one-on-one witness and Bible exposition, Philip baptizes the Ethiopian, setting in motion the birth of the first African church. As an encore, Philip is whisked away, instantaneously transported, Star Trek style, to Azotus.

Yet still, in Acts 8, Philip is not called the evangelist.

It's not until we catch up with Philip again in chapter 21, a couple of decades later, that he's given that title. Why? The book was written in one go. Why wait till halfway through before giving one of your major characters their proper title? Particularly when their major starring role has come and gone?

For my money, there's significance here. It seems to me that Luke holds fire on labelling Philip 'the evangelist' until Caesarea, because it is in Caesarea that Philip finally grows into the fullness of the evangelist's role and ministry. Gifting is not the same as ministry. You can't have the ministry without the gifting; but you *can* have the gifting without the ministry. In Acts 6 and 8 there is amazing gifting, but the role of evangelist is more than that. There's individual brilliance on show, but not necessarily the empowering or preparing of saints for service that Ephesians 4 requires. It's not about charisma and competence; it's about connection and context.

When Philip was transported from his desert encounter to Azotus, he proceeded to preach his way to Caesarea. Nearly twenty-five years later, he's still there. Now correct me if I'm wrong, but that doesn't seem like the archetypal hit-and-run evangelist. That's some serious long-term investment. And that's where the biblical role begins to be fulfilled.

Put it another way. Philip crops up in Acts 21 because Paul comes to stay with him as he visits the highly influential Caesarean church. Now think what would happen if Paul, the most significant Christian leader in the world, came to stay in *your* city. Suppose he wanted to find out how the city church was doing, catch up on the issues, strengthen the saints. Who would you put him up with? Who would you trust to represent the church to him? Who could speak most lovingly and most knowledgeably about what was happening? Who would have the best grip of the big picture, the strongest connection to the most areas of church, the wisest insight?

Put your hand up if it's the evangelist ...

For most people that's the nightmare scenario. Wouldn't you be ever so slightly worried they'd be a tad critical about church, a wee bit ignorant of some of the health issues, a little disconnected from large tracts of church life? That is, if they're at home in the first place.

With the Caesarean church it was obvious. Which senior leader loves the church more, knows the church more, represents the church more than Philip? He's the evangelist: it's a no-brainer.

It's either that, or he was the guy with the biggest house and the flashiest pool.

Look up the word 'evangelist' in a dictionary and you'll see Philip's big-toothed face smiling back at you. His family life is exemplary – he has four daughters that prophesy even though they are not old enough to be married. He's long-term. He's at the centre of church. He's got an established track record. He's a man of proven character who's carried weight at senior level. He's not above the church, he's not at the edge of church, he's not under the church. He's absolutely engaged at the *heart* of church.

Now wouldn't you want an evangelist like that on your team?

3. *The essential evangelist*

Finally, let's look at 2 Timothy 4, the third mention of the term evangelist in Scripture.

> But you, keep your head in all situations, endure hardship, *do the work of an evangelist*, discharge all the duties of your ministry.
>
> For I am already being poured out like a drink offering, and the time has come for my departure. I have fought the good fight, I have finished the race, I have kept the faith. Now there is in store for me the crown of righteousness, which the Lord, the righteous Judge, will award to me on that day—and not only to me, but also to all who have longed for his appearing (2 Tim. 4:5–8, italics added).

This is an unusual one. Paul's writing the last chapter of his last letter. I can never read it without feeling desperately moved. Paul knows his time is up, he has maybe weeks left. But he can look back on a life of service and say with confidence that he's fulfilled his calling. His work here is done. Now it's up to Timothy.

With his final words to his favourite son, Paul charges Timothy to discharge all the duties of his ministry. But then he throws in *that* word, evangelist. 'Do the work of an evangelist.' And this is what makes it unusual, because Timothy is not an evangelist. He's a senior pastoral leader.

You've read the letters to Timothy. They're full of practical, nitty-gritty instructions on theology and teaching and church practice. They're about what kind of leaders to choose, how to combat heretical teaching, what kind of clothes to wear. They're about lifestyle and values and church structures. They're about worship and prayers and public Scripture readings. They're about materialism and social care programmes. They're about morality and leadership. For goodness sake, they're even *called* the Pastoral Epistles.

Timothy was the sometimes timid young man that Paul left to take over the senior leadership of the Ephesian church. He's the archetypal diffident young pastor. And yet Paul's final words to him instruct him to 'do the work of an evangelist'. Why is this? It's not as if Paul doesn't know what he's talking about. He identified and defined the ministry in Ephesians 4, and stayed with the ultimate example in Acts 21.

Again, we have to get to grips with the nature of the ministry to understand the thinking. 'Evangelist' is not primarily a gift, but a *role*. And it's a role that is utterly essential to the health and growth of the church. It's about equipping, empowering and resourcing the body of Christ to make disciples. It's about producing mini-heralds, developing effective witnesses, releasing the members to proclaim the message.

And that ministry is simply indispensable.

What Paul is saying here is that the role of evangelist is so uniquely vital it needs to be categorically owned by senior leadership. In effect, the role is too important to just leave to the evangelists. Timothy was to keep this role firmly in his sights, to make sure that it happened in church life, no matter what.

This is good news, albeit challenging. There are many, many church leaders out there scratching heads and wondering exactly how to source the kind of biblical evangelist we've outlined above. The bottom line is, if you're the leader then *you* take the responsibility for the role. It's part of the duties of your ministry.

That's the challenging bit. The good new bit is that there's plenty of evangelistic gifting and potential out there. If you have just twenty people in your church, the chances are that at least one of them has evangelistic potential. If you have less than twenty, then one's not far away.

Identifying the evangelist's role

Let's put things together and see how they relate.

In a nutshell, the role and ministry of the evangelist needs to find expression in church life in three distinct areas.

1. Essential core evangelistic leadership

The Timothy passage is a revelation because it locates responsibility for evangelistic work right at the heart of senior leadership. Regardless of their gifting or personal inclination, those charged with the responsibility of church leadership have to take on board the duties of evangelistic ministry. They have to ensure that every saint is equipped for outreach service, that every member is a missionary, that every individual is empowered to bear fruit.

It's not unusual to find churches in which outreach has been hived off to an evangelism sub-committee, or sub-contracted to an outside agency.

This is a big mistake.

When you do this you abdicate one of the leader's core ministry duties. You communicate that outreach is an adjunct, an optional extra, rather than a core concern. By all means, spread the load. But outreach is the one area that you dare not delegate away.

We'd recommend strongly that one member of the senior leadership team takes on particular responsibility for outreach in the church. The outreach process is so challenging, and a joined-up strategic approach can be so involved, that it's vital to have a dedicated key leader who can devote time and energy to it. It may not necessarily be the overall leader of the church, but it does need to be someone at the senior level.

A key leader for outreach may not see themselves as particularly gifted in evangelism, but as long as they see the need, and are willing to take on the 'Timothy injunction' to fulfil that role, then you have something to work with. It then becomes the responsibility of this key leader to draw in the rest of the team, to relate to and lead those with gifting at grass roots, and to oversee the mobilization of every member as a missionary.

Outreach has to be at the heart of every element of church life, considered in every decision, factored into every plan. Someone senior needs to have their eye on the ball, to understand all components of the outreach plan, and to facilitate the process.

Evangelistic leadership has to be at the absolute core. Don't let it escape your senior team, or you'll *never* build a culture of outreach.

2. *Empowering evangelistic ministry*

Despite the cheap gags at the beginning of the chapter, the role of the preaching evangelist is still needed in local church life. In many cases, such an individual will not be part of your church, but they can be partnered with. I've spent the last twenty years serving the church as an evangelist, sometimes in an itinerant role, but latterly in a more focused, regional role.

The evangelist has a ministry to both herald and equip. They can bring a vital cutting edge to your outreach activities, bringing to bear their gifts in helping others commit to Christ. They can also help to inspire, motivate and empower your members in outreach. When Philip visited Samaria, the overall effect was 'great joy.'

Still, they tend to be focused types. You're best off using them in a focused way.

3. Engaged grass roots evangelistic leadership

These are the ones to use liberally and comprehensively in church life. These 5 per cent characters hold the key to unlocking the growth potential in your church. They are the ones that can influence, inspire and equip the church at small group level. They may currently be over the church, at the edge of the church, or even under the church, but it *is* possible to engage them at the heart of the church, at the grass roots.

It's possible to nurture and develop an effective, corporate evangelistic ministry through certain key members in your church. Given time, vision and energy, you can engage these gifted people to fulfil this essential, empowering role.

In the next chapter we'll show you how.

Questions for leaders

1. Essential core evangelistic leadership

- Have we as senior leaders been guilty of abdicating our evangelistic leadership responsibilities? Is outreach identified as a core leadership concern, or have we delegated it away?

- What would it mean for us to fulfil the Timothy injunction to 'do the work of an evangelist?'

- Who in our senior team is the most appropriate person to fulfil the outreach key leader role?

2. Empowering evangelistic ministry

- Do we make strategic use of those with a recognized gift of evangelist in our church? Are they being engaged to bring a cutting edge to our outreach activities?

- Is the ministry gift of evangelist being used effectively to 'equip the saints' in our church?

3. Engaged grass roots evangelistic leadership

- Who can we readily identify within our church as being evangelistically gifted? Do we see them operating over, at the edge and under the church, or are they effectively engaged at the heart? Are we talking to them and, most importantly, listening to them?

- In which individuals do we see the potential to provide grass roots evangelistic influence and inspiration for our church? What might the challenges be?

Chapter 5

Growing from Grass Roots

'The best argument for Christianity is Christians: their joy, their certainty, their completeness. But the strongest argument against Christianity is also Christians – when they are sombre and joyless, when they are self-righteous and smug in complacent consecration, when they are narrow and repressive, then Christianity dies a thousand deaths.'

Sheldon Vanauken[1]

Once we grasp the truth that a proportion of the members of any given church have evangelistic ministry potential, the possibilities become very exciting. Instead of only looking *outside* the church for evangelistic answers, we begin to also pick up on the wealth of untapped gift *within* the church.

As we noted in the last chapter, it's usually easy to recognize and engage the classic evangelist. We're used to the charismatic, preaching, trans-local evangelist. The Evangelist with a capital 'E', if you like. Their ministry and input is vital to the health and growth of any church.

---

[1] Sheldon Vanauken, friend of C.S. Lewis, author *A Severe Mercy* (San Francisco, CA: Harper, 1992).

But in our experience the secret to effective, long-term, sustainable growth lies in recognizing and engaging the input of the evangelistically minded members within the church already. These are the grass roots operators, the potential catalysts and influencers, the 5 per cent of the population. These are the evangelists with a small 'e'.

Partners in the gospel

A number of years ago when I helped to lead a large church in the south-east of England, we began to grapple with the issue of engaging latent evangelistic gift within the church. We were asking the questions: where does the evangelistically gifted member fit in regular church life? How can we draw the best out of them? How do we pull them into the centre of church life, as well as allowing them to operate on the margins?

At the time we were getting a steady trickle of seekers visiting our main Sunday service, and we decided that it would be appropriate to offer a weekly gospel invitation. We determined to engage some of the more obviously evangelistically motivated members to help. It was as much about drawing them in, as it was about reaching out to seekers.

Tom was a case in point. Subtlety and grace weren't exactly his strong suit, and he'd often clashed with leaders. He was the typical 'bear hunting' archetype we joked about in the first chapter. But for all his rough edges, he was undeniably passionate about outreach, and he was genuinely gifted. I'd seen him 'at the edge' of church, and I'd seen him get frustrated and end up 'under' the church, barely holding on to his own faith. Now we wanted to see him effectively engaged and at the heart.

The service where we'd asked Tom to give the gospel invitation was led by David, one of the senior pastoral leaders. He introduced Tom and handed him the microphone. What happened next surprised us all. Instead of the tub-thumping, 'manic street preacher' we were expecting, a different Tom turned up. He was nervy, apologetic and overwhelmed. He rambled his way through the appeal, stopping every few moments to take huge, panicky gulps from a bottle of water. It was painful.

Finally, when he invited people to come forward for prayer, there was nothing but silence and an embarrassed cough. Somewhere, in the distance, I think I heard a bell faintly tolling.

It was then that David stepped forward and put his arm around Tom. 'I'd like to underline Tom's invitation,' he said. 'You need to listen to this man. He knows what he's talking about. He knows what it's like to be delivered out of despair, and he knows what it means to be given a new start.'

And, just like that, the floodgates opened. People came forward for prayer, people dedicated their lives to Christ, one of my own close friends became a Christian. It was just wonderful.

There's a strategic partnership between pastoral leadership and evangelistic ministry that can be incredibly fruitful for the church. I saw it demonstrated powerfully that night, and I've seen it worked out in a hundred different ways since. The pastorally gifted and the evangelistically gifted can cooperate in a mutually supportive and beneficial way. This book itself is a practical outworking of that principle.

It's the evangelist that helps the church engage with the world; it's the pastor that helps the evangelist engage with the church.

Identifying the influencers

If you want to shape a culture of outreach effectively, then it's vital that you engage the input and influence of evangelistically gifted people already in the church. The problem, though, is they don't all look like Tom. They don't necessarily conform to a stereotypical picture.

So how do you identify these key potential influencers?

Here are three things to look for: gifting, potential and commitment.

1. Gifting

We're primarily looking for individuals within the church that have some form of evangelistic gifting. But it would be a mistake to simply cast around the church looking for the person with a bundle of tracts in one hand, a bull horn in the other, and a mad glint in their eye. The evangelistic gift is varied and broad, and expresses itself in many different personality types.

It's best spotted by looking at three signposts – motivation, track record and connections.

Motivation: The easiest way to spot an evangelistic gift is to follow a person's motivations. What gets them excited, what releases energy for them, what makes their eyes shine? When thinking about any given individual, ask yourself these questions

- Do they express a heart for those outside church? Do they often verbalize a desire to see people come to faith?

- Do they get excited and energized by evangelistic initiatives and try to encourage others to get involved?

- Do they particularly enjoy and respond to ministry/ motivation from evangelists visiting the church or speaking at larger events?
- Do they get excited by stories of people coming to faith, and pass those stories on to others?
- Do they find involvement in a vision or programme of outreach more rewarding and engaging than involvement in regular church activities?
- Do they ever express dissatisfaction that the church isn't 'doing more' to reach out to people on the outside?
- Do their eyes light up when you talk about mission and glaze over when you mention maintenance?!

Track Record: Scripture tells us that we recognize the tree by the fruit. Being excited about crumble doesn't make me an apple tree. Apples do.

Here are some questions to help you consider the fruit of an individual's life

- Do they have a history of sharing their faith with people?
- Have they brought people to church meetings or events in the past, even when it's not particularly that appropriate?
- Have they been involved in trying to reach people for Jesus in their workplace, neighbourhood or relationship network?
- Have they volunteered for church outreach activities in the past, such as Alpha, community surveys, short term mission trips, etc?
- Do they have significant close relationships with people outside church?

- Do they naturally tend to gravitate towards visitors at church meetings, trying to draw them in and welcome them?

- Can they relate naturally to non-believing people? Are they at home with non-believers, and are non-believers at home with them?

- Have they successfully used special 'red letter' occasions – such as their baptism, child's dedication, wedding etc – to invite a crowd of non-believing friends and family to church?

- Have they ever played a significant role in others coming to faith?

Connection: It's a cliché to say that birds of a feather flock together. But that doesn't stop it from being true. Ask yourself these questions about a person's connections

- Have they aligned themselves with ministry opportunities at the open edge of church – like hospital/prison visiting, youth and schools work, mums and toddlers, street teams, chaplaincy, etc?

- Do they 'buy in' to outreach events outside the local church, like regional or national campaigns?

- Do they tend to make alliances/friendships with people from other churches who have a clear vision for those outside church – particularly at work or in their local community?

- Do they naturally identify with and gravitate towards others with a clear evangelistic heart/gift? Are they part of a group with a particular outward looking focus?

Not all these questions will apply to any one individual, but if you find yourself answering more questions with a 'Yes' than a 'No', then there's a good chance that you've got yourself someone with a real evangelistic gift.

2. Potential

Unfortunately being gifted, in and of itself, is not enough.

Raw talent or heart is no guarantee that an individual will be effective in helping release long-lasting growth in a church. The role that needs to be developed here is one of a catalyst, a fire starter who can help instil and inspire a heart for outreach in others.

Some evangelistically gifted people can actually inhibit outreach in others. They can present such a strong model of outreach, specific to their own personality and gifts, that others feel disqualified because they're not like that. Some, for whatever reason, may lack credibility with ordinary members in the church. Others simply lack the ability to bring people along with them.

What we need are those with the potential to *influence* others, to empower them, to help train and equip them. In short, they need to be able to lead, as well as be evangelistic. That's why we call them grass roots evangelistic leaders.

If you have to choose between someone with genuine leadership potential but no strong evangelistic gift, and someone with evangelistic gift but no real leadership potential, you choose the leader every time. Ideally, you want some measure of natural evangelistic gift as well, but if a person has a mission mentality, and if they can embrace outreach values, then you can build on that.

The key is the influence and engagement with the church at grass roots, and for that leadership potential is vital. Here are some questions to help identify that potential

- Does this person have the potential to influence others positively? Do others take them seriously and respect them enough to listen to them?

- Does this person have the potential to communicate ideas clearly and confidently in a small group setting?

- Does this person have a 'bias for action'? Are they able to be proactive?

- Does this person have the capacity for enthusiasm? Is their enthusiasm infectious, rather than off-putting?

- Does this person have the potential to take a lead in small group life, particularly in the area of that group's outreach?

3. *Commitment*

Finally, we're looking for people at the grass roots who can commit themselves to a long-term process, and who are willing to serve the church, so that others might be empowered, resourced and released.

Creating and sustaining a culture of outreach, even at small group level, is a real challenge. You need people willing to take responsibility, to give themselves to the vision, to do whatever it takes. You need those that you can rely on, that you can train and equip, that you can build with.

These last questions probably need to be considered with the individuals themselves, as part of the enlisting process

- Is this person committed to the church – her mission, health and growth – or simply to their own ministry and fulfilment?

- Is this person willing to serve others and see them succeed in reaching their friends, neighbours and colleagues?

- Is this person willing to accept a role given to them by the church leadership in facilitating church growth at a small group level?

- Is this person willing to commit themselves to seeing the process through – not simply when all is encouraging, but also through the inevitable setbacks, disappointments and struggles?

Information, attitudes and value

Here's a saying; 'Information is taught; attitude is caught; but values are bought.' It's a nice piece of folksy wisdom that underlines the fact that our true values always cost us. Your culture is the outworking of the values that you *really* believe, not the ones you *say* you believe. They're the ones that you pay the price for – in time, energy, effort, prayer, example and, yes, money.

A culture of outreach comes as you cultivate outreach values, and in turn it nurtures, encourages and propagates those values. Developing evangelistic leaders at grass roots gives you people who can model outreach values for the church. Instead of merely a 'top down' approach, you gain a 'bottom up' one too, making you twice as effective.

And yet you've also got to give attention to the *information* and *attitude* part of the saying. We've talked about the need for every member to understand outreach principles, but this requires someone to teach them. Who better to help than your grass-roots evangelistic leaders? Again, it gives you the potential for both a 'top-down' and 'bottom-up' approach.

Like many of the facets of discipleship, outreach is as much caught as it is taught, and it's here where your grass-roots operators are particularly crucial. An outreach attitude can be wonderfully contagious. Having key

individuals sprinkled throughout church life who are able
to influence those around them, letting their natural heart
for the lost rub off on others, is enormously beneficial to
any growth strategy. It's this that turns a dry programme
into a breathing reality.

So we're looking for evangelistic leaders at grass roots
who can model outreach values, teach outreach principles,
and infect others with an outreach attitude.

Over the last few years we've created a systematic
process for developing these evangelistic leaders. It consists
of two years of teaching, mentoring, resourcing and on-
the-job training. We call it the Church Growth Academy.
In a variety of situations it's proved its worth in engaging
people with evangelistic and leadership potential, and
setting them loose to find a place of fruitfulness and
fulfilment in church life. It's far from the only way of
working out these principles, but if you're interested you
can find out more in Appendix B. For now let me give you
two stories.

The first took place when we launched the Church
Growth Academy in a particular church. After the first
session, a young lady came up and spoke to us. 'Listening
to the teaching I couldn't stop crying,' she said. 'At last, I
thought, someone understands me. Someone feels about
church the way I do!' The second story happened in
exactly the same way, but in a different church. This time
the comment came from a young man who said, 'For the
first time, I see how I fit into church. I've got a role that I
can fulfil. I feel like I've just been given permission to be
myself.'

There are gifted people in your church who have a vital
role to play in helping stimulate an outreach culture at
grass roots. They are motivated individuals who will help
lead and inspire others. They will come alive when given
the opportunity to take the initiative in outreach, to teach

others and model values. They may not be evangelists with a capital 'E', they may need patient shaping and strategic investment. But they are a gift to the church from the risen Christ, just the same. Give them a mandate, give them training, give them a role. Help them see how they can serve the evangelistic strategy of the church in the areas where they're already involved – in their home groups, in the youth work, in community projects. Draw them together regularly so that they can stimulate and learn from each other. Trust them and set them tasks, lead them, engage them.

The outreach community

Grass roots evangelistic leaders are absolutely key, because without them it's extremely difficult to create and sustain an outreaching community. This community aspect to outreach has been largely under-emphasized in our modern church, but it is a very strong motif in Scripture. Alongside the power of the individual worker and 'soul winner', we need to unleash the huge power of the attractive community.

This brings us back to our Mark 2 starting-point: outreach people that group together to carry the needy to Jesus. Communities like this don't happen by accident. They don't form just because you tell them to, or because you teach them the right principles. It takes key culture formers at the grass roots to really establish things.

In chapter 3 we looked at what Jesus *modelled* for the individual disciple, now it's time to look at what Jesus *taught* his followers about the outreach community. Time and again, Jesus taught his disciples about the *process* nature of salvation, he commanded them to *witness* to what they'd seen and heard, and he encouraged them corporately to be a visible sign, an attractive community that the whole world could *access*.

1. Process

Jesus used parables that constantly emphasized the natural, organic nature of the kingdom. The kingdom of God, he said, is like a field that a farmer sows with seed. Given time and process the field inexorably produces a crop, first a stalk, then an ear, then the grain within the ear. The kingdom is like a mustard seed that grows from small beginnings into a mighty tree; it's like yeast that works its way through a batch of dough; it's like wheat and tares growing in a field, like a sower going to sow.[2]

We examined this when we looked at the Parable of the Sower and the John the Baptist Principle in chapter 3. Preparation is key, because the growth process of salvation can only take place when effective ground work has been done.

The problem is that, for most of us, seeing the process through can be tremendously difficult. As the parables imply, the kingdom grows in secret ways not immediately apparent to the naked eye. It's easy to think nothing's happening, it's easy to get discouraged. It's not always easy to keep going, to keep serving, to keep loving, when you're not sure if you're actually making any impact.

Thus, the first thing you need grass roots evangelistic leaders to do is to *support*. We have to provide support systems for each church member in their individual outreach. The ideal place for this is at the small group level.

---

[2] Parable of the Field, Mark 4:26–29; Parable of the Mustard Seed, Mark 4:30–32; Parable of the Yeast, Matthew 13:33; Parable of the Weeds, Matthew 13:24–30; Parable of the Sower, Matthew 13:1–23.

We need to make sure that outreach support, as well as general pastoral support, is on the agenda for each small group in the life of the church including the leadership team. Each person should know who their fellow group members are reaching out to, how it's going and what the issues are. Prayer for each other's non-believing friends should be a regular part of the agenda. There needs to be a periodic injection of encouragement, inspiration and biblical input. When there are good stories, and encouraging moments, these need to be fed back and celebrated.

It doesn't take much to work out that in order for this to happen, your grass roots operators need themselves to have regular inspiration and encouragement. If outreach values are a natural part of what makes them tick, then this shouldn't be too difficult. But it's vital to make sure that we are regularly inspiring and energizing our key culture formers, who in turn go back and motivate, strengthen and support the small groups they're a part of. Allow people to voice their discouragements, to rejoice in their successes and to draw strength from one another.

Relational outreach can be a tough, long haul. It makes all the difference knowing that we're not doing this on our own.

2. Witness

You don't have to look very far to realize that Jesus didn't just *teach* his disciples to be witnesses. He *commanded* it.

When it comes to the proclamation of the message, the preferred biblical method is the testimony of the real life witness. Witnesses literally speak of what they have seen, heard and experienced. The word witness occurs around seventy times in the New Testament, in contrast with the three times that the word 'evangelist' occurs. The whole weight of Scripture is tipped towards ordinary believers telling their story.

Jesus promised his disciples power from the Holy Spirit to witness in his name.[3] The impact of the every day, empowered witness would ripple out from where they were, right across the world. The commission Jesus repeatedly gave his disciples was to go and proclaim good news, to share their stories, to herald the kingdom.

It's a mistake to think that relational outreach is about replacing words with actions. I never did like that Francis of Assisi quote: 'Preach, and if absolutely necessary use words.' Frankly, nobody's that good! It seems fairly plain that Jesus commanded us to share good news in ways that people could hear and understand. Clearly Jesus used words, and he calls us to do the same. Friendship, loving relationships, incarnational service simply give us the most appropriate context in which to speak.

Jesus constantly urged his disciples to 'Go and tell.' The practical issue at hand is that many Christians lack the confidence to obey that command. Even mature believers are often ill-equipped to bring others to faith in Christ. We lack confidence in the gospel, we lack the skill to share it with creativity and relevance. We're inhibited in our ability to speak naturally and effectively about our faith in Christ.

In this instance, the role that grass roots leaders can fulfil is to *teach*. Training people up to succeed as witnesses is another thing usually best done at small group level. It's one of those areas which is as much caught as it is taught. Principles and guidelines need to be imparted,

---

[3] Acts 1:8: 'But you will receive power when the Holy Spirit comes upon you; and you will be my witnesses in Jerusalem, and in all Judea and Samaria, and to the ends of the earth.'

but it's the experience and confidence that makes the difference. And that's best modelled by a peer.

Grass-roots evangelistic leaders need to be equipped and trained themselves. They need to be confident in telling a simple salvation story, dealing with difficult questions, understanding how to communicate effectively, knowing how to help a person commit themselves to Christ. They then need to be given a context and a mandate to pass on that teaching, those skills and attitudes, to others at small group level.

Training for witnesses needs to be drip fed into church life over a period of time, not necessarily crammed into an intensive course. (You can find more information and ideas on this in Appendix C.)

3. *Access*

This is where the power of the community comes in to its own, for as much as Jesus enjoined us to 'Go and tell', he also encouraged a 'Come and see' approach.

When Jesus called his discipleship community 'the light of the world' (Mt. 5:14) his point was that a visible community of believers is incredibly attractive to the outside world. The issue in Matthew 5 is not that we somehow struggle and strive to attain 'light-ness.' The issue is *placement*. We are unequivocally the light of the world already, just by virtue of being the body of Christ and filled with his Spirit.

The question is: *where* are we being the light? How visible are we? Are we under a bowl, or on a stand? Are we in a prominent position, can our good deeds be seen by others, are we high profile in our relationships and togetherness?

That's why Jesus prayed for our unity and for our love, one with another. He told us that it would be by our *love* that men would know we were for real; it would be by our *unity* that they would know that he was from God. Apologetic argument and theological debate have their place. But it's a loving, united, Christ-centred community that is the biggest sign post to salvation there is.

The sad truth is that, for most church communities, if people on the outside want to see our love and our unity and our hope then they need X-ray vision. It all happens behind closed doors, in closed meetings, behind church walls. It's a light, but there's no way that anyone can really see it. There are no access points.

Now, as we stated in chapter 2 when we first examined the Matthew 5 passage, it's up to the leaders to set the tone, to orientate the church, to take the initiative. But to see that culture effectively grow and permeate every level of church, you need to engage your grass roots evangelistic leaders. Here, their role is to *stimulate.*

Having key culture formers on the ground means that someone is looking to open up access points, ways in which the world can experience the church community. We often do social things together, but how often do we open those up to those outside the church? You'd be amazed at how powerful it is when groups of believers simply include their friends in social events, and allow them to see the body in action. Too often we overreach ourselves, trying to invite people to come along to a spiritual event, like a service or a seeker course. It's so much easier and more natural to first draw them in through the rhythms of shared life and friendship.

A couple of days ago, I spoke at a church evening service where a good number of people ended up responding to a gospel invitation. One of them was the sister of one of the guys in my home group. Her first exposure to church was four months ago when she was invited to a pub lunch and Sunday walk with a couple of dozen church members. From that moment, after being initially resistant, she became intrigued with the church community, and things developed from there.

What could be more natural for us than worshipping together, then eating together and walking together? How easy it is for us to extend invitations to those that we're praying for and building bridges with. We shouldn't be surprised when people end up being attracted and drawn in by the community. It's the most natural thing in the world.

But here's the point: it wouldn't have happened unless someone with influence stimulated it. Someone had to have the idea, the creativity, the initiative. Left to their own devices, small groups in church life will invariably default to maintenance and introversion. But if we can infiltrate them with agent-provocateurs who will stimulate an outward focus, awaken an outreach instinct and provide creative and simple access points, then we'll start to go places.

That's what it means to be a city on a hill. Make no mistake: a visible, attractive church community will draw seekers like moths to a flame.

Building the culture

Let's tie things together with nine steps for building a culture of outreach.

1. *Catch the vision*

It starts with leadership. We have to see things for ourselves, become energized by the possibilities and grasp the potential. Everything is created twice. Before it can be created in the real world, it must first be created in your heart.

2. *Evaluate the reality*

We have to start with actual reality, not an idealized version of it, the things that are actually happening and the values that people really hold. Take stock, examine the values that you are actually 'paying for.' Ask questions of your members and your fellow leaders. Conduct an 'outreach audit' of your church, combining formal evaluation with casual observation. Be honest with yourself and be clear about your starting-point.

3. *Set the goals*

Begin to create a strategic plan and break things down into simple, measurable goals. Your ultimate vision may be for each member of the church to be able to bring their friends to faith, but an initial goal might simply be to ensure that each member has at least one non-believing friend.

4. *Generate the motivation*

As a rule, it's impossible to grow something without changing it, and it's impossible to change something without causing it pain and discomfort. People generally hate change, they resist it. In order to change a culture you have to provide the energy of motivation. One of the most effective ways of doing this is to breed a sense of godly dissatisfaction with the status quo. It's only as people come to feel uncomfortable with the way things are – the lack of fruit, the ineffectiveness of witness, the embarrassing contrast with biblical teaching and models – that they will be willing to pay the cost of change and growth.

5. *Provide the teaching*

The truth sets us free. It's not enough to tell people the vision, we need to give them the tools, the principles, the hands-on training. Sprinkle missional teaching right through the programme, from the main venue to the living room.

6. *Model the example*

Sorry, but you can't lead what you don't live. It starts with you and your example. Leaders hold the keys to what happens in church, for better or worse. People will follow who you *are* and what you *do*, not what you *say*. In the words of Stephen Covey, 'You can't talk your way out of what you've behaved yourself into.'[4] Remember, values are bought. Here's where you start paying.

7. *Engage the influencers*

We've talked at length about grass roots evangelistic leaders, but there are plenty of other key influencers in church life. Start a quiet revolution. Enlist the help of the catalysts in your congregation. Burn the vision into them, take them into your confidence, engage them to play a part. If you can then encourage them to do the same with others, then you've got yourself a people's movement.

8. *Structure the values*

Build outreach into the framework of church life. Find slogans that express the values, write them into the mission statement, create language that encapsulates the vision. If creative prayer for non-believing friends, outreach-themed Bible studies, and open social events are woven into the regular programme, then outreach will soon become second nature, the way we do things round here. More on this in chapter 9.

---

[4] Stephen Covey, *The 7 Habits of Highly Effective People* (revised edn; London: Simon & Schuster, 1999).

9. *Reinforce the process*
   Culture creation is a circular process of steady improve-
   ment, and it's here that you underline positive behaviour
   before taking things to the next level. Pass on good
   stories, focus on good practice, praise and reward good
   examples.

The key to good communication is not intensity, but
consistency.

Pulling it all together

Let's summarize.

A culture of outreach is the only real way to effectively
deliver long-term, organic growth. It taps into the latent
evangelistic potential of a church and allows people to play
to their strengths. It is best created through a combination
of 'top-down' evangelistic leadership, teaching and vision,
with 'bottom-up' grass-roots evangelistic influence.

Leaders need to understand the fundamental principles
of outreach. For the individual disciple, it's about the
incarnational dynamic: people bring people; it's about
loving people by meeting the needs they feel; and it's
about engaging the power of God to overcome obstacles
in a person's life, particularly through consistent, focused
prayer.

For the community of believers it's about understanding the process nature of outreach and supporting
one another through it; it's about engaging witnesses
who are equipped, trained and inspired to share their
stories; most of all, it's about allowing the world to see
and experience the Christ-centred community, creating
natural, appropriate and engaging access points.

The secret weapon in establishing an outreach culture
is the engagement of evangelistic gifts at grass roots. It's

about identifying and enlisting the contribution and influence of grass roots evangelistic leaders, equipping them, validating them and engaging them to empower the body of Christ at the cellular level.

All this requires vision, strategy and structure. This is not an overnight solution, and you can't achieve it with an off-the-shelf package. This requires investment, energy and commitment over the long haul.

It's also not enough to just motivate and equip people, either. Leaders have to provide the frameworks and programmes to support, facilitate and power the outreach process. The good news is that this is surprisingly easy to do, and we'll devote the last chapter of the book to showing you how.

But first it's important that we understand with clarity and depth what conditions are necessary to make sure that growth can genuinely happen. An outreach strategy cannot simply be bolted on to a church. It has to be integrated and assimilated into the very fabric of church life. To succeed, we have to look not just at church *culture*, but at the very essence of church *health* itself. We have to move from content to context.

In these last chapters we've set out something of a road map, a way forward for effective outreach and growth. But all the maps in the world are of little use if the vehicle you're driving has engine trouble.

It's time for us now to lift the bonnet and take a look at what's underneath.

Questions for leaders

1. Grass roots evangelistic leaders

- Which members of our church do we think best fit the profile for grass-roots evangelistic leaders? How do they shape up in terms of evangelistic gifting, leadership potential and commitment to church?

- In what ways do we think we could begin to engage, develop and resource these individuals to impact the rest of the church at grass roots?

2. Process

- How well do we think that the members in our church understand the 'process' nature of biblical outreach? To what extent do we emphasize the importance of *preparation* in the outreach process?

- How effective are we at *supporting* our members in their relational outreach? Is this built into our small group structures and woven into our culture?

3. Witness

- How well equipped are our members to communicate their faith to others? How effective have we been at teaching and training people to be witnesses?

- How can we engage grass-roots evangelistic leaders to help teach others? Do they themselves need equipping first, and if so, how?

4. *Access*

- How accessible are we as a community to those outside the church? Are there easy access points at every level of church life, from small group to gathered congregation?

- How can we engage our key culture formers to stimulate an attitude of openness and welcome?

5. *Building the culture*

- What is our vision for a culture of outreach, and how are we doing in reality?

- How can we use the nine steps to begin to establish a stronger outreach culture in our church?

PART TWO

Creating a Culture of Outreach
Getting the CONTEXT right

DAVID LAWRENCE

Chapter 6

Churches with Winning Ways

'Expressing the life of Christ through the local church
... that ultimately is both the goal of every church and
the right measure of its health.'

Robert Warren[1]

In Part One of this book Philip has focused on how to develop a culture of outreach in your church by releasing the evangelistic potential at leadership and grassroots level. In Part Two I want to take a step back from that specific focus and explore the larger issues relating to the health of a local church.

Experience has shown that even the healthiest evangelistic strategies will soon wither and die if grafted onto an unhealthy church. In the natural world and in the world of local church, health leads to growth; ill-health inhibits growth, and maybe even leads to death.

As mentioned earlier, for nearly eighteen years I was a leader in a church that saw conversion growth each year. It may not have been revival by South American standards, but it felt good to be around people who were accepting Jesus as Lord for the first time.

---

[1] Canon Robert Warren and Dr Janet Hodgson, *Springboard Resource Paper* 2.

During these years the peaks of my 'job satisfaction' as a leader were the baptismal services where new followers of Jesus would publicly confess their faith in God; Father, Son and Spirit. They were always exciting occasions. We encouraged the people being baptized to share simply in their own words why they had got to the point of wanting to follow Jesus. It was always deeply refreshing – and often very moving – to hear these new Christian disciples tell their own story of finding faith, often using language that was completely unaffected by theological accuracy or Christian piety.

I vividly recall Tracey's testimony. Tracey was in her twenties and in her place of work had first met and then started going out with Ian, a lapsed Christian who had some links to our church. Around that time, Ian began to rediscover his own faith and, as a consequence, Tracey herself was progressively challenged about her own standing with God. Eventually, after a long struggle (including walking out of the Alpha weekend away) Tracey made her own Christian commitment.

As she came to be baptized on the day in question, she nervously stood at the microphone to explain to the gathered crowd (which included non-Christian close family members who were suspicious of what was happening to her!) why she had decided to follow Jesus. Her opening comments (and I quote) were, 'My sister and me went to church when we were kids, but we got kicked out because my sister farted in choir practice.'

I'm not sure that any of us had actually heard the vernacular for 'breaking wind' used from the front in a church service before, and its groundbreaking use now caused an interesting reaction. The non-Christian guests didn't blink an eyelid; it was after all a normal English word as far as they were concerned. The church members – to their credit, I think – broke out into gales of laughter.

It got me thinking about just how much church had changed since my upbringing in an evangelical free church, somewhere in the south of England. I can only imagine the impact that Tracey's opening sentence would have had back then. The deacons would have gone white and Aunty Dot would have adjusted her hearing aid and inquired '*What* did she say?'; the minister would quite possibly have stopped the baptism altogether on the ground that Tracey had just 'demonstrated her lack of preparedness for such an event' and the congregation ... well the congregation would have lapsed into a stony-faced silence of the sort that follows an England football team penalty shoot-out.

All that, as I say, is what I *imagine* would have happened: the one thing that I am certain about is that absolutely no one at all would have laughed.

The church that lost its way?

This incident is perhaps a very small pointer to some of the seismic shifts that there have been in the church scene in the UK between the Swinging Sixties and the Nervous Noughties. The church has changed and for many the church has disappeared from their radar screens altogether. The figures of church decline are by now well rehearsed – and although as we noted in chapter 1 there are pockets of the Christian church in the UK that are growing, the overall trends are still downward.

Reflection on the reasons for the disappointment of the 1990s' evangelistic efforts has identified a number of reasons for it, amongst them the indication that an agenda which focuses on *growth*, but ignores fundamental issues of *health* is doomed to fail.

A churchless faith?[2]

In desperation, some are giving up on 'church' altogether and seeking pathways of faith outside of organized Christian communities. Whilst we can perhaps understand the frustration – and sometimes hurt which leads people away from organized expressions of Christianity – theologically it is hard to defend such a position.

God (who himself is God-in-community; Father, Son and Spirit) always intended to create a world-blessing *community* in his image. It was Adam and Eve's mandate to 'fill the earth' with a loving *family* and Abraham was to be the father of a God-honouring *family* whose mission was to be a *'great nation'* and whose God-attentiveness would result in 'all peoples on earth' being blessed. In Jesus' commissioning of the twelve disciples, we see the deliberate act of reconstituting a new Israel around himself as King.

The New Testament epistles offer only *corporate* images of Christianity: living stones being built together; body parts forming one whole; branches grafted into one tree and sheep identified as one flock, for example.

The church indeed is intended to be the first-fruits of that new *society* which God is calling into being; 'a nation called by God to be the bearer of the meaning of cosmic history to the rest.' It is not surprising, then, that 'building the faith community seems to be central to what the writers of the epistles saw as the work of evangelism'[3]

---

[2]　The title of a book by Alan Jamieson which explores the pathways of faith explored by people leaving Evangelical, Pentecostal and Charismatic churches in New Zealand. He himself admits that his title is an oxymoron. See Alan Jamieson, *A Churchless Faith: Faith Journeys Beyond The Churches* (London: SPCK, 2002).

[3]　Robert Warren, *Building Missionary Congregations* (Church House Publishing, 1995), p. 1.

for ultimately it is our lives that give credibility to our words.

There are doubtless many varieties of the form of the church, but to try to pursue faith in Jesus whilst denying fellowship with his brothers and sisters is to act outside of God's redemptive purposes.

Whose job is it?

For those who accept the need to 'do church' as part of their Christian calling, an important question is 'Who builds church?' There are two equal and opposite errors that we can fall into at this point.

Error 1: Fatalism – The 'Wait-on-God' approach

The first is a kind of *fatalism* that concludes that if God wants his people to grow and the lost to be found then he is more than capable of achieving these goals by himself. The church's position is one of quietism and pietism; waiting on the Lord in faithful, prayerful obedience until Revival (with a capital R) comes.

Error 2: Activism – The 'Work-Harder' approach

The second error is a kind of *activism* rooted in a belief that 'It's all down to us' and that if we just try harder, sacrifice more deeply, organize more events, hire more evangelists and community workers – and especially youth workers(!) the kingdom will surely come. If fatalism says 'It's all down to God', activism assumes that 'It's all down to us': the former leads to introspection; the latter leads to exhaustion, and neither necessarily results in effective outreach.

A more healthy perspective is that of the apostle Paul who saw a balanced division of responsibilities between Christian workers and God: 'I planted a seed, Apollos watered it – but God made it grow.' For the church in Corinth to grow, Paul accepted that there were some things that he could do to influence that; he could plant some gospel seeds; he further recognized that he needed to work in partnership with others who had complementary gifts if there was to be growth in Corinth. But ultimately Paul was happy to concede that only God can cause a church to grow.

The horticultural imagery is helpful because it is so obvious. The preacher's tale about a keen gardener who was talking to a passer-by makes the same point in a different way.

The passer-by was praising the beauty of the garden. 'Isn't it wonderful to see the beauty of God's handiwork so splendidly laid out?' he enthused. The gardener scratched his head thoughtfully before responding, 'Well it is,' he conceded, 'but you ought to have seen it when God had it to himself.'

God has graciously – perhaps even surprisingly – refused to go back on the 'Plan A' that he put into effect in Eden. He still chooses to enter into meaningful partnership with his children as his primary tactic for engagement with his world. This means that, on the one hand, we need to be humble before the Holy and pray as though everything depended on God; but on the other hand that we need to be committed before the Creator, and work as though everything depended on us.

The notion of being God's 'partner' in church-building reminds us that, in the words of Stuart Murray, 'healthy churches ... do not just happen ... We need processes and practices that challenge unhealthy attitudes and behaviour, train our reflexes and build community.'[4] Before we look

---

[4] Stuart Murray, *Church After Christendom* (Milton Keynes: Paternoster, 2004), p. 166.

more closely at some of those processes and practices here are three more things *not* to do.

Error 3: Historicism – the 'We've-always-done-it-this-way-before' approach

'Historicism' is the belief that if we keep doing what we've always done, somehow we'll get better results next time around. There may indeed be a time for maintaining previously unsuccessful practices. Jesus, after all, commanded his fishermen to have another go at casting their nets into the lake, even though they had been totally unsuccessful up to that point. If Jesus says 'Just do it' then 'Just do it', no matter what you have caught so far. But apart from that exceptional divine word of command, to keep running activities or programmes that have borne no evangelistic fruit for the last ten years could be a sign of methodical madness.

Nearly every major piece of research into church health identifies being 'open to change' as an identifiable quality of healthy, growing churches. Research carried out in the Diocese of Durham into churches that were bucking the trends of decline and actually seeing some encouraging growth showed, amongst other things, that they were likely to be congregations that were not just repeating history but were willing to 'face the cost of change and growth.' Similarly, Christian Schwarz's international research into the differences between churches that were experiencing growth and those that were in decline, identified a church's willingness to shed unhelpful aspects of their historical skins and adopt new 'functional structures' as one of his eight core Church Health Characteristics.[5]

---

[5] Robert Warren, *The Healthy Churches' Handbook* (London: Church House Publishing, 2004), p. 31; Christian Schwarz, *Natural Church Development Handbook* (Moggerhanger: BCGA, 2002⁴), p. 28.

Error 4: Plagiarism – The 'Willow-Driven-Cellsong'
approach

The next common mistake to be wary of as we join in
partnership with God's outreach to the world is Plagiarism.
The Willow-Driven-Cellsong approach basically hopes that
if we do what the church across the road (or even better,
across the Atlantic) has found to be fruitful, we will get
the same results.

Now please don't misunderstand: it is only arrogance
that stops us learning from one another, and as a church
leader I was indebted to the models and methods which
others had developed, tested and generously shared.
However, whilst we may indeed learn from others, it is
usually impossible to actually copy them. Every local
church is unique – because the church is the people, and
every church has different people! Different resources,
different cultures, different settings, etc all militate against
a simple transposition of church A's methods into church
B's culture.

Error 5: Pastoralism – the 'When-we're-good-and-ready'
approach

We call the final common mistake we would like to high-
light Pastoralism. Many leaders are distracted from their
primary role of paying attention to core issues of church
health by the constant demand for pastoral care from their
members and the weight of 'nitty-gritty' organizational
details that are required to maintain the status quo. The
vision-sapping 'Three P's' – pastoral problems, premises
issues, programme maintenance – dominate the agendas
of individual leaders and leadership teams. You don't have
to go looking for these things; you don't have to schedule
them in your diary or list them on your meeting agendas:
they will hunt you down, often in packs. The resultant

temptation is always to sort out the 'internal maintenance' issues in order to clear the decks for the day of visionary and missional thinking.

Let me give it to you straight; such a day never comes.

The roof will always leak (or the foundations sink); there will always be a programme of activities to maintain (who *is* on the rota for coffee next week? and have they remembered to get the Fairtrade stuff in?) and there will always be pastorally demanding people around who may well need constant propping up until Jesus comes back (and that's just the leadership team).

Somehow, without allowing the building to crumble, the programme to collapse or the cases of pastoral need to be neglected, leaders *must* make some efforts to free themselves to focus on the core issues of church health.

I vividly recall when I first met Terry. Terry is the leader of a church with whom I work as a consultant, and I now count him as a friend. When we first met I asked Terry to list the tasks that he felt were core to his role as key leader of the church. The list was staggering! We covered three large sheets of flip-chart paper with a range of tasks that spanned hospital-visiting to hedge-cutting and Bible studies to boiler maintenance. When we reflected on the list we saw (or rather Terry saw) that he was so busy 'pastoring' that there was no mention on his list of core tasks of planning for activities which were targeted beyond the church community. It was also a bit of a shock to Terry to see just how little of his time was actually spent on building up individuals in their discipleship. He had fallen victim to pastoralism and he and the church (never mind the surrounding community) were suffering as a result.

To summarize: the church in the UK is in a state of flux; old certainties, practices and models for mission have all been cast into the melting pot. The issue seems to focus on how we as leaders and members of the church can enter into a partnership with God to form healthy churches, which almost instinctively and naturally grow: health is the necessary platform for growth. However, we have suggested that health does not necessarily come through adopting the tactics of fatalism, activism, historicism, plagiarism or pastoralism.

A model of health

So where then *might* we look for our yardstick of church health? What *can* we use to inspire our self-identity as 'church', to create our core values and to motivate our mission? Our simple suggestion is that we peer back beyond the findings of contemporary research (or else we could just become faddists), beyond historical models of church and mission (lest we become historicists), and even initially *back beyond the New Testament epistles* to root our ecclesiology in the mission and practice of Jesus himself.

The church is after all, by definition, centred on Jesus Christ. *The* key church health principle is therefore Christocentrism: the church is as healthy as it is Jesus-like. I do not think that it claims too much to say that all of the first-century churches saw themselves as 'Jesus' churches, their lives individually and corporately being radically reoriented by the claim that Jesus of Nazareth is now Lord of the cosmos.

The Jesus-theme is everywhere. The Jerusalem church was comprised of those who were baptized in the name of Jesus Christ, who devoted themselves to the apostles' teaching (which clearly focused on Jesus Christ) who witnessed miracles in the name of Jesus Christ and who, when they met, celebrated the central Jesus-event in bread and wine.

The good news carried by the evangelists was the good news of Jesus Christ and the churches that they planted were 'those sanctified in Jesus Christ,' 'those who call on the name of our Lord Jesus Christ,' 'the body of Jesus Christ,' 'the faithful in Jesus Christ' and 'the saints in Christ Jesus.' Jesus was the goal of their growth, the example to be copied, the 'cornerstone' on which they were being built together and the 'capstone' by which they were held together. Jesus was pictured as the exemplar church pastor and the exemplar church member.

It couldn't be clearer, could it? The first Christians were Jesus-people. But why? Surely because they (or at least, in the first instance, the apostles) knew enough about a real Jesus, who spoke clearly enough to be heard and understood and whose intentions were clear enough to be injected into the very life-blood of the communities formed in his name.

The focus of the church was the faithful continuation of the life and mission of Jesus Christ.

The Master Builder

So what can we learn from Jesus about healthy church? Well, according to Matthew at least it was Jesus who took the word 'church' – *ekklesia*[6] – and chose it to summarize his mission. The first time that the word *ekklesia* appears in the New Testament is in Matthew 16 where Jesus, responding to Peter's faith-statement ('You are the Christ, the Son of the living God') responds by announcing that 'I

---

[6] The word denotes the calling together of people for a common purpose. It was used of secular authorities and also of the Jewish synagogues. Scholars dispute which use should be given more weight in its Christian setting.

will build my church, and the gates of Hades (death) will
not prevail against it.'

It is important to note that '*hades*' denotes the world of
the dead and not 'hell.' Jesus was not here promising that
the church would be triumphant over demonic powers, but
that it would be an *eternal* building project which death
itself – including his own death and that of his disciples
– would not interrupt. The church is unfinished business
as far as God is concerned.

So – how did Jesus himself go about fulfilling his stated
objective – and start building church, the new household
of God?

It would be unrealistic to expect a tidy ecclesiology to
emerge within Jesus' own lifetime. The notion that he,
the carpenter's son from Nazareth, was reforming God's
community around himself took a bit of getting your
head around within first-century Judaism. Tom Wright
points out that such a worldview shift inevitably left his
disciples 'with more or less muddle, uncertainty and
failure', as they tried to 'put what he said into practice'
and subsequently sought to use his teaching 'as the basis
for their self-understanding as the renewed community
of YHWH's people.'[7]

However, having acknowledged that, there do seem
to me to be three core elements to Jesus' expectation of
his 'church' which emerge clearly, both from his teaching
and actions.

1. Discipleship

Firstly, when Jesus began to reform God's community
on earth, he deliberately made himself the centrepiece.
'Follow me' was the challenge; ditch the old ways of being

---

[7] N.T. Wright, *Jesus and the Victory of God* (London: SPCK), p. 318.

human that you have picked up from your culture and upbringing and remodel your lives around me.

The theological shorthand for that realignment is 'repentance': small wonder then that the gospel writers could summarize Jesus' offer of life with the words, 'The Kingdom of God is near. Repent and believe the good news!'

We will develop this much more in the next chapter, but for now we simply note that Jesus' 'church-building' was rooted in the summons to *himself* and a special relationship with him characterized by repentance and discipleship.

2. *Community*

The second core of Jesus' church, however, went beyond calling individuals into radical relationship with himself. On one memorable evening he shocked those who were following him by adopting the servant's role and washing their feet.

Whilst they were still processing what was going on, Jesus did another surprising thing: he gave them a commandment. Jesus, who had spent so much of his ministry apparently redefining or even challenging common interpretations of the commandments, now offered them a new one: 'A new command I give you: Love one another. As I have loved you, so you must love one another. By this all men will know that you are my disciples, if you love one another' (Jn. 13:34–35).

For Jesus, the claim of love for him wasn't enough. Love for him must be expressed in authentic discipleship: and *discipleship must be proved by loving other disciples as he had loved them*, i.e. by humble, selfless service within the discipleship community.

It is in individuals committed to Jesus – and in the communities that they form – that God lives by his Spirit. It is the presence of the Spirit that makes the church more than a human workforce. Orthodox theologian John Zizioulas puts it like this

> The Spirit is not something that "animates" a church which already somehow exists. The Spirit makes the Church *be*. ... We can therefore understand the church as being "instituted (by Christ), but ... constituted (by the Spirit)".[8]

The second core identity marker of Jesus' church was to be a committed, loving community life, formed as individual disciples choose to love one another as Jesus has loved them. This community life becomes the 'temple', made of living stones in which God lives by his Spirit.

We shall look at some core aspects of church-as-community in chapter 8.

3. *Touching society*

Thirdly, these communities of Spirit-empowered Jesus-followers were not to view their identity as a haven from the world – but rather as hope for the world. They, like Jesus himself, were charged with the commission to be light for the world, and instructed to act in society like salt, giving the world a fresh flavouring and a much needed preservative. This third world-facing aspect of church is the focus of chapter 9.

Disciples of Jesus, committed to one another for the sake of the world; this is our understanding of the kind of church that Jesus started to build – and the sorts of churches that we are commissioned to continue building. We could represent this kind of 'church as Jesus intended' with a simple diagram where church is represented by the area of overlap at the centre of the diagram.

---

[8] John D. Zizioulas, *Being As Communion* (New York: St Vladimir's Seminary Press, 1985), p. 132, 140.

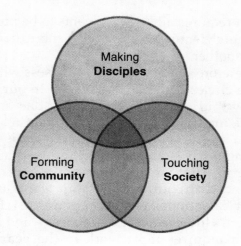

We believe that these three circles represent the core identity markers – the irreducible minimum – of what it means to be the church of Jesus Christ. Church leaders who embrace this model will immediately have a framework for assessing everything they do by asking themselves 'How do our activities contribute to making disciples, forming Christian community or reaching out to touch society?' If on reflection anything that we give time, effort or money to actually does not contribute to one of the three core elements of church, then let's stop doing them!

All three elements are important to be 'church.' If you are just making and nurturing disciples you could be a training college maybe, but not a church.

If you are just a great big happy Christian family, you could be some sort of Christian club perhaps, but not a church.

If you are just passionately working to make Jesus known in society then you'd be an excellent mission agency, but not a church.

Church requires all three elements to be present, and healthy church requires all three elements to be in balance with one another.

It is therefore important to try to assess whether any one of the circles dominate the others. In our work, we commonly find that each church has one area where they are doing well – and one where they are relatively weaker. In such a situation the temptation is always to keep doing what is already working well and turn a blind eye to what isn't. This is not a good idea. We recommend that church leadership teams undertake regular (at least annual) periods of prayerful reflection on their church's life in each of these areas – and especially ask which requires most work in the year that lies ahead.

How healthy are we?

The church in the UK is changing – maybe even emerging – but whether your church is a mega-church or a simple church; whether you meet round the Lord's Table each Sunday or the kitchen table each Tuesday; whether you're neighbourhood based or network based, these three circles offer a simple, universal way of keeping the main thing, the main thing.

In a time of reassessment and reconfiguration we believe that evangelistic church leaders can do no better as they work in partnership with God in his eternal church-building project than to keep returning to these three core questions which define the essential elements of church health

- How well are we making disciples of Jesus?

- How well are we forming community-life?

- How well are we functioning (individually and corporately) as salt and light in God's world?

In the next three chapters we shall explore each of these core identity-markers in more detail.

Chapter 7

Church and Discipleship

'The big mountain for the church is to breed radical disciples – Christians who are willing to serve brittle and broken people rather than themselves, and who seek to be transformed so that they can transform society.'

Michael Moynagh[1]

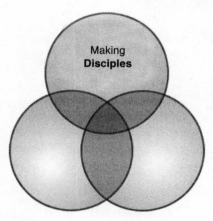

In Part One, we've been talking about creating a culture of outreach in your church. We've stressed the importance of evangelistic leaders at the heart of church life, about

---

[1] Michael Moynagh, *emergingchurch.intro* (Oxford: Monarch, 2004), p. 43.

identifying and releasing grassroots evangelistic leadership and about mobilizing every single member of your church in effective outreach. The goal is to empower the church to participate in Jesus-style outreach: to seek and to save the lost.

Evangelistic leaders, grassroots evangelistic leaders, mobilized members and newly saved lost friends may be very different people, but they do all have one thing in common: the call to be a disciple of Jesus Christ.

Church consists of disciples of Jesus Christ but I guess most people in the UK still live with a vague understanding of church as being what you get if you add together a special building + minister + services.[2] As long as you can identify all three elements you have a church; if any one goes missing people generally can't get their bearings and are suspicious that you may not be a proper church at all.

Having led a church which has never had ordained leadership and never owned its own building (though we had plenty of services!) I can vouch for the fact that you have to work very hard to establish your 'credentials' as authentic Christians if any part of the equation is missing. In the town where our church took root, even the other church leaders initially referred to us as 'the outsiders' and local people had no means to tell us apart from any other religious sect or cult.

But should the nature of our buildings and the presence of an ordained minister running services be the authentic marks of church? We have already suggested not. Rather we would rewrite the equation, drawing on Jesus' own

---

[2] Or to use Robert Warren's language reflecting a different view of ministry 'Church = Building + Priest + Sunday Services.' See Robert Warren, *The Healthy Churches' Handbook* (London: Church House Publishing, 2004), p. 84.

apparent practice and expectations as he began to build his church, as church = disciples + community + impact on society.

In this chapter, then, we want to think about the first part of that equation and reflect on the business of being and making disciples.

We all know that Jesus' commission to his disciples was that they should go into the world and make more disciples, in other words reproduce in others what Jesus had put into them. His challenge was not that they should plant churches, for without disciples you cannot have a church (according to our definition at least); churches are what happens when disciples join their lives together and so making disciples was to be the first step in expanding the Jesus movement from Jerusalem to Rome and beyond.

The church by this way of looking is that body of people who are seeking to live out together a personal acceptance that Jesus is Lord. That definition may leave a lot of ecclesiological loose ends hanging for some, but though the church may be more than that, it is never less than that. To talk about 'church' in any meaningful way, there must be at least two or three who together agree that 'Jesus is the Christ, the Son of the Living God': that confession is the only sure foundation to build church on, the rock on which church is built.

If *disciples* make disciples, then the first challenge for evangelistic church leaders who wish to see their con-gregations (be they two or two thousand in number) bear evangelistic fruit is to ask, 'Are we as a congregation developing the kind of disciples who attract people to Jesus?'

As we've now said a number of times, 'outreach' cannot be bolted on to a church as kind of occasional optional extra; it has to be intrinsic to the way the church thinks about itself. Every part of church life will impact on our ability to reach out into the world, and none more so than the quality of our individual discipleship.

What follows are therefore ten foundational ideas about discipleship in the local church.

1. *Discipleship not conversion*

According to Mark's Gospel, Jesus himself is the good news (Mk. 1:1). His life, death, resurrection, ascension, Lordship and return form the variegated unity of the gospel.

Gospel truth is therefore not a series of statements about the cross that we assent to in order to get a ticket to heaven; gospel truth is a Person who we follow in order to gain a passport to life (a present *and* future reality). People who believe the former are likely to be content with a view of salvation that leads people to accept certain truth-statements, pray a prayer affirming their acceptance of the 'ABCD of salvation' and then assume that God has tucked an invisible ticket to heaven in their back pocket.

Job done: convert made.

This kind of 'conversion' can however lead to a static understanding of a change of position – changing one's state from 'lost' to 'found' or 'sinner' to 'saint' with little expectation of movement on from that point. Once I stood here in a world of sin; now I stand over here in a world of salvation.

Discipleship on the other hand is a dynamic concept which is to do with learning, following and acting out one's love for Jesus. Discipleship is relational and transformational. Once I made sense of life by creating my own values and doing what I wanted but now I make sense of life by adopting Jesus' values and doing what he wants. I used to live to please myself but now I live to please him.

This is a key difference between the concept of conversion and that of discipleship.

Conversion can actually be a very selfish thing; a consumer exchange. I want something (forgiveness, place in heaven, peace) and so I'll pay the sinners prayer and hopefully get what's on offer. Discipleship, on the other hand, (rightly understood) is Jesus-centred and cross-shaped; in the first place it's about attraction to Jesus and then about what I must give up in order to enter a relationship with Jesus as Lord.

To change the metaphor, to ask people to convert is to ask them to jump ship from the doomed sinking raft that they had been becalmed on in mid-ocean and join the lifeboat of salvation – which offers a far safer place to be becalmed. The only difference is that previously you were doomed to sink but now you will stay afloat for all eternity. There's no movement in the mean time, just a confident hope that when God eventually blows on the ocean you will now stay afloat, whereas your previous raft would have sunk.

To invite people to be a disciple, however, is to offer them not a lifeboat but a power boat. Certainly they need to understand that their current life is sinking, but God invites them to abandon it for a life of new potential and power, driven by his Spirit and captained by an on-board Jesus.

Maybe we shouldn't draw too big a wedge between the two images, but to think of our main aim in evangelism as 'making disciples' rather than 'counting converts' does in fact begin to transform what we are doing as we reach out.

Rather than being concerned to count converts, perhaps we should heed the counsel of Dallas Willard again and first learn 'to weigh our members, not just count them.'[3] He goes on to explain that 'the popular model of success involves counting the ABC's – attendance, buildings and cash.' How do we know if we are being successful in outreach? Easy: just count the converts, measure the building and weigh the offering.

If leaders focused instead on 'weighing their members' growth in love, joy, peace, long-suffering, gentleness, goodness, kindness, and so on', the growth of church would be largely taken care of as those maturing qualities would overflow into the surrounding world of family, friends and neighbours. It's how Jesus did it: concentrate on transforming a few and send them out to transform others.

Church built on converts is too easily becalmed. Church built on disciples has a dynamic about it which keeps flavouring the worlds of its members with the aroma of Jesus. It's about discipleship not conversion.

2. No discipleship: no outreach

As mentioned above, over the years that I have led a church, baptismal services have always been a special thrill; for me, they were the icing on the cake of leadership responsibility. The best bits of those services were the stories that people told of coming to faith. I'll be honest here: there was always a little bit of me that wanted to hear these stories go something like this

> I was a wayward, dissolute wretch until by accident (or so I thought at the time) I found myself passing this church on a Sunday morning. The doors were open and I heard the sound of singing which drew me inside. As I entered,

---

[3] M. Shelley (ed), *Leadership*, Summer 2005, Vol. XXVI Number 3 (Illinois: 2005), p. 23.

everyone sat down and I shuffled into the back row just as David rose to speak. I was immediately gripped by his ministry. The powerful effect of his words drew me right into the presence of God. Questions that I'd carried for years were all answered and I felt that my aching heart was strangely warmed within me as it was filled to overflowing with love, joy and peace. At the end of the service I left before anyone could speak to me. It wasn't that I didn't want to speak with anyone but I couldn't do so because of the tears of repentance and joy running down my cheeks. I could barely wait until the next Sunday when I could return and hear some more; as soon as David rose to speak I just knew that I had to commit myself to Jesus Christ as my Lord and Saviour. And so I am here today to be baptized as a sign of the new life that has grown in me since David planted those seeds with his faithful preaching of the gospel.

I never ever heard anything remotely like that in a baptismal testimony. What I more usually heard was a tribute to one or more members of the congregation, whose love for Jesus had been sufficiently alive and strong that it had acted as a magnet, drawing the non-believer towards Jesus. In fact the very first person we ever baptized put it this way: 'I first saw the love of Jesus in the eyes of my next door neighbour.'

This is entirely consistent with the findings of contemporary research which sees the vitality of individual church members' faith as a critical constituent of overall church health.

Christian Schwarz, for example, lists the presence of what he calls 'Passionate spirituality' as one of his eight key church health indicators. Here is what he found

Our research indicated clearly that church development is dependent neither on spiritual persuasions (such as charismatic or non-charismatic) nor on specific spiritual practices (such as liturgical prayers, spiritual warfare, etc.) ... The point separating growing and non-growing churches ... is a different one, namely: 'Are the Christians in this church "on fire"? Do they live committed lives, and practise their faith with joy and enthusiasm?'[4]

Passionate disciples are the magnet which God seems to use to draw people into his arms.

Dallas Willard describes the link between making disciples and outreach with this striking statement: 'The way to get as many people into heaven as you can is to get heaven into as many people as you can: that is, to follow the path of genuine spiritual transformation or full-throttle discipleship of Jesus Christ.'[5]

No discipleship: no outreach.

3. *Disciples are passionate lovers*

Have you ever wondered why on earth a bunch of Galilean fishermen should jump ship and follow the carpenter's son from the village across the hill? What ever did he offer them to seduce them away from their security, families and income? What convinced them to swap fishing trips for discipleship?

It would appear that Jesus offered a stark choice to those he called.

To the fishermen it was 'Your nets or me.'

To Matthew, the Rich Young Ruler and Zacchaeus it was 'Wealth, or me.'

To the following crowds it was 'Die to your own agenda or don't kid yourselves you're a disciple at all.'[6]

---

[4] Christian Schwarz, *Natural Church Development Handbook* (Moggerhanger: BCGA, 2002), p. 26.

[5] Dallas Willard, *Renovation of the Heart: Putting on the Character of Christ* (Leicester: IVP, 2003), p. 25.

[6] Mark 1:14–18; Luke 5:27–28; 18:22; 19:8–10.

The call to discipleship was a radical call *away* from the things that had previously filled people's horizon (building a business, making a profit, getting ahead in life) and a call *to* Jesus. To be sure people may have spent more or less time getting to know Jesus before the challenge was issued – but the challenge was always there.

The technical word for that shift of allegiance is 'repentance' and it was at the heart of Jesus' gospel. The kingdom of God is here – he proclaimed. In other words, there is a new King in town – a new Ruler who can straighten life out, put broken things back together and defeat the root of evil in the world. How do you get in on this King's agenda? 'Repent and believe this good news.'

The new life of the kingdom is only received by submission to the King; or to use different language: the old 'lords' that had dominated our lives – the things we got out of bed for and gave our lives to – need to be submitted to the new Lord, Jesus Christ. It's an either-or thing. 'Choosing one path invariably required rejecting other paths, and it is impossible to walk on more than one path at once if you are actually trying to get somewhere.'[7]

Jesus put it like this: no one can serve two masters. Either he will hate the one and love the other, or he will be devoted to the one and despise the other … (Mt. 6:24). Too often the gospel invitation has been to accept Jesus as 'Saviour' but not as 'Lord.' This has led to converts who welcome the free gift of salvation but baulk at the costly cross of discipleship.

So what is the dynamic force that draws us away from the tyranny of the old masters – which in many cases we have served for a long time and more or less learned to

---

[7] Brian Walsh and Sylvia Keesmat, *Colossians re:mixed Subverting the Empire* (Milton Keynes: Paternoster, 2005), p. 170.

get along with – and adhere to a new 'Lord'? The simple answer to that is 'love for Jesus.'

Jesus offered *himself* to his followers: 'Follow me' was the invitation, 'cross and all.' The apostles were called in the first place 'to be with him' (Mk. 3:13) before they were to be trusted with reaching out. The broken apostle Peter was to be recommissioned for pastoral and missional work, not on the basis of his qualifications, past track-record (which was patchy at best) nor the ardour of his commitment to do better in the future, but simply on his love for Jesus.

The only thing that will make sense of 'church' is love for Jesus and a commitment to him as Lord, which results in giving all for him. It's true for evangelistic leaders, grass-roots leaders and all members of our churches.

Jesus is the gospel; our challenge as church leaders is how to keep offering him as the good news and not substituting us, our churches or our reductionist doctrines in his place. *Helping people to keep their love for Jesus alive is one of the most basic and important pastoral tasks that we evangelistic leaders face.*

4. Make disciples ... baptizing them

How is this step into the Lordship of Christ made? Becoming a disciple of Jesus may well be something that people want to weigh up for a long time. They may want to hang around his twenty-first century followers and watch what is going on, hear what is being said – and crucially, weigh up the lives of those who claim to follow. That's fine; it's good and healthy to 'relate before repenting';[8] it's

---

[8] I prefer this phrase to 'belonging before believing' because I am not convinced that you can 'belong' to Jesus and his church in any real sense prior to repentance. You can, however, certainly relate to Jesus before repenting.

what Jesus experienced. He always seemed to welcome the crowds who wanted to see what all the fuss was about.

However, Jesus was careful not to allow the following crowds to imagine that they were actually 'with him' just because they hung around him. In Luke 14 Jesus challenged 'followership' by pointing out that authentic 'discipleship' entails the carrying of a personal cross – a daily turning from self to God and others.[9]

It was, it seems, not Jesus' way of seeing things that you could 'belong' to his discipleship group before shifting allegiance from the consumerist mindset of 'following' for what I can get out of it, to the cruciform mindset that understands that true life in the image of a giving God is only discovered in the giving away of life.

Now this transition, from follower to disciple needs to be marked in some way so that all can know the boundary has been crossed. When Jesus gave the commission to 'go into the world and make disciples' he mandated that the boundary crossing moment should be marked by an act of baptism.

In baptism people who are abandoning the old masters that so dominated their lives are sealed 'into' a new identity – that of God himself. They are baptized into the name of the Father, Son and Spirit, and thus reunited with their identity, lost in Eden, as children of God.

Baptisms are great; wet'n'wonderful celebrations of new life, new identity, new hope – new everything in fact. They are a dramatized multi-sensory statement to the individual and all onlookers that the old has gone, and the new has arrived. More than that, they are the start of a new life in which Jesus walks alongside and lives within the baptized person. 'I am with you always' is a wonderful assurance

---

[9] Luke 14:25ff.

that this new identity doesn't slip when we do (more on this below). Rather, in this new Jesus-bent life, God the Father deigns to dwell by his Spirit, offering internal resources for obedience, transformation and service.

The challenge of this for church leaders is in what follows on from baptism – the other part of 'how to make disciples' in the Great Commission is 'teaching them how to obey everything' that Jesus had commanded his disciples. It is to this that we now turn.

5. *Make disciples ... teach them to obey*

Following Jesus as Lord had immediate – and not insignificant – implications for the first disciples. The very word 'disciple' just means 'learner' and certainly Jesus expected his disciples both to learn what a Jesus-centred life would look like and expected them to live out what they had learned.

The Sermon on the Mount is perhaps the most condensed form of the teaching that Jesus offered his disciples. Intentionally assuming the seated position of the Rabbi, Jesus called his disciples to him and taught them what radical realignment of life would be necessary, should they choose to live with and for him. 'You have heard this ...' but 'now I tell you this ...' is the repeated theme of the Sermon. Jesus clearly felt it to be important to transmit a body of information about what life under his Lordship would look like. Yes, there was continuing teaching throughout their years with him – life-long learning if you will – but at the sharp end of starting to follow him Jesus wanted to paint a picture of what discipleship would mean.

It is interesting to compare the 'curriculum' of some contemporary first-steps discipleship courses with Jesus' own curriculum in the Sermon on the Mount. We find a contrast at several key points.

- *Jesus' curriculum covered the whole of life, not just its 'religious/spiritual' aspects.* Spirituality and lifestyle are indissolubly linked by Jesus. There is no dualism or sacred/secular, spiritual/material hierarchy. Teaching on marriage and divorce sits alongside prayer and fasting; relationships with others (especially enemies) are deemed as important as one's relationship with God. Discipleship is about re-learning to live life as though Jesus was me; how would he treat my enemies, my wife, my financial situation. The Sermon on the Mount reminds us that we are not trying to produce academic theologians who can cross and dot all of their doctrinal *t's* and *i's*, nor are we trying to produce compliant, conforming church members but people whose *whole lives* are remoulded around Jesus of Nazareth.

- *Jesus' curriculum challenged attitudes not just actions.* Indeed, his challenge was that unless you change the heart of bad attitudes at the root of the tree, you will never bear good fruit for the kingdom. In our society, where people imagine that actions and attitudes can be divorced (e.g. politicians who expect to be trusted in public despite cheating in private), Jesus' holistic view that heart and action, fruit and root cannot be divorced will surely lead us to examine our discipleship programmes to discover where the 'heart' work takes place.

- *Jesus' curriculum expected transformation through obedience.* The use of the word curriculum should not deceive us into believing that Jesus was simply interested in giving new instructions and filling his disciples' heads with new information – or even new dreams. No. Jesus expected that his disciples would actually put this teaching into practice and begin to 'live the dream.' The Sermon on the Mount is not a tantalizing description of what life will one day be like when God is in charge; rather it is a challenge to live today as though God is indeed already in charge. The whole Sermon ends with the challenge that blessing awaits those who not only hear the words, but put them into practice (Mt. 7:24–27).

In John's Gospel we encounter a similar thought: 'you shall know the truth and the truth shall set you free', said Jesus. Transformation and liberty; what a promise! But how is that liberty attained and that truth known? The preceding verse gives the answer. 'If you hold to my teaching, you are really my disciples. *Then* you will know the truth and the truth will set you free.'[10]

Authentic discipleship is about liberty through obedience, or as Jesus put it 'now that you know these things, you will be *blessed if you do them*.'[11]

Hearing and learning are not enough; it is those who obey – who put the teaching into practice – whose life foundations are transformed from sandy subsoil to storm-resistant rock.

6. Disciples need disciplers

When my youngest son, Tim, left school he wanted to go into agricultural engineering and was fortunate enough to be offered an apprenticeship with a local company. The company's apprenticeship scheme was a mixture of on-the-job experience working alongside experienced engineers as they fixed everything from lawn mowers to combine harvesters, and a weekly placement at a college where

---

[10] John 8:31, emphasis added.
[11] John 13:17, emphasis added.

theoretical knowledge was passed on. From day one Tim was getting his hands (and everything else) dirty, but in a structured, supported environment where he could learn from those who had already been around the blocks (and pistons) a few times.

Imagine, however, if on the first day at the company Tim had been sent out to fix the combines himself with no support, or training! That would have been scandalous and ridiculous, since everyone knows that apprentices, by definition, are learners and that as such they need mentors, supervisors and teachers offering good examples for them to learn from and follow.

Apprenticeship is a very healthy image for discipleship, in fact the Greek word for disciple could also mean 'apprentice.' 'Discipleship' doesn't happen automatically and naturally. To lead someone to faith and then to just hope that they will know how to work out the implications for themselves is as unreasonable and irresponsible as expecting an engineering apprentice to work out how to fix the broken engine.

Disciples need mentors, advisors, supporters – and crucially good examples of Christian living – to develop their own understanding of what the Jesus-is-Lord life looks like.

Discipleship – like an engineering apprenticeship – may require some 'classroom education', but it also requires this real-life life-support system that only comes through personal relationship with a disciple who has travelled the road for a bit longer than the new disciple.

Jesus of course spent three years modelling life to his disciples; Paul was brave enough to offer his own life as an example for his churches to imitate; Peter urged leaders to provide 'examples of Christian living' to their flocks.[12]

---

[12] John 13:14,15; 1 Corinthians 4:16; Philippians 3:17, 4:9; 1 Peter 5:3.

Wherever you look, the assumption is that discipleship doesn't just happen; it needs to be developed.

This need not be a 'professional' minister; in fact one of the best informal disciplers that I know is an elderly German lady called Margot who just opens her heart, her home and her Bible to friends on her council estate who are coming to faith in Jesus. She didn't think of what she was doing as mentoring, and she wasn't part of a formal church mentoring programme, but her own faith naturally overflowed into the lives of these friends and neighbours in such a way that they were encouraged in their own walk with Jesus.

However it is done, whether formally as part of church structures or informally in friendship networks, church leaders are responsible for ensuring that every disciple is in fact being 'discipled.'

7. Disciples fail

I've yet to meet anyone who learned something new for whom occasional failures and mistakes were not part of the learning process. My wife teaches piano in the room beneath my study. Each week the same children come and play the same pieces and, at first at least, make the same mistakes: Sophie struggles with her G harmonic minor scales and Alex comes a cropper eight bars into Jazz for Imps.

If my wife struck Sophie or Alex off her student list every time that Sophie missed the E^b (again) or Alex's fingers refused to follow his brain to bar 9 then neither of them would ever mature into proficient musicians. However, like all good teachers, she understands that our mistakes are what we learn from and that making mistakes is an integral part of the learning process.

If only we'd make the same allowances for disciples!

I grew up in a Christian setting in which it was assumed that when you converted to become a Christian, your life was straightened out at that point. Coming to Jesus meant victory over the world, the flesh and the devil – so if any of those formidable opponents still seemed to be exerting an active influence on your life, your conversion was called into question (another problem with the concept of conversion).

How different from the relationship that Jesus enjoyed with his disciples. Peter is the classic case of hero-to-zero and back again, and again, and again – from providing the rock on which Jesus was to build church, to being the mouthpiece of the devil, from a loser by the fireside in a courtyard to the lover by the barbecue on the beach. Talk about inconsistent. Yet was there ever a time when Peter was not a disciple; a time when Peter was not stumbling after Jesus, even if occasionally overcome by his own temperament and fears? I think not.

Discipleship is a life-long adventure and it is only at the end that we shall hear the final verdict on our following. In the journey itself there will be times of failure and disappointment; when we let not only ourselves down but those close to us as well. And here is precisely where we need to understand that it's okay; God can cope with our failures on the discipleship path.

Psalm 139 reminds us that God is not caught out by our human frailty and flakiness. He 'knows how we are formed, he remembers that we are dust.' How important it is that we remember the same thing about ourselves and those that we are encouraging along the discipleship path with Jesus.

Frances was a heavy drinker, occasional drug user and husband beater before coming to faith in Jesus. With a background of abuse like hers it was not surprising that she turned to drugs to blot out the pain. Furthermore, it is not surprising that committing herself to follow Jesus as Lord was not going to instantly undo the pain and the coping mechanisms that she had accumulated over the years. Slowly, however, she began to learn what it meant to follow Jesus and she found increasing freedom from the things that blighted her life. However, there were still some Sunday mornings when she arrived for church a little the worse for wear after a heavy session the night before. Why did she come? Because, she says, 'I knew you wouldn't condemn me.' And why wouldn't we condemn her? Because we understood that her discipleship journey (like ours – and like Peter's) was going to be an up and down journey in which failure was part of the learning programme.

8. HDJDI? not just WWJD?

WWJD (What Would Jesus Do)? It's a great question; sometimes the answer is clear, sometimes not.

Caught in a sinking ship; WWJD? Of course! Walk across the water – or maybe command the tempestuous waves and wind to subside. WWJD? Easy: problem solved.

Of course knowing what Jesus would do *is* a great place to start, but beneath the WWJD question is another, deeper question: HDJDI?

How Did Jesus Do It?

The disciples themselves soon picked up the WWJD agenda. A father comes running to them. 'Help, my lad keeps fitting and throwing himself into the fire. No-one can help him, but I heard that you guys might have the answer.'

'Oh help', think the disciples, 'WWJD?'

The answer soon came; they knew that Jesus would deliver the boy of whatever was oppressing him. So they strode into action; they struck the pose, said the words and

– nothing! Despite the fact that they knew WJWD, they couldn't do it themselves.

To their relief (or was it embarrassment?) Jesus appeared and took the situation in hand. He did what Jesus did (as they had done) but with a very different effect. Why?

'Jesus, WCWDI?' (Why Couldn't We Do it?)

The answer (depending on the gospel you read it in) is because whilst the disciples knew how to adopt the pose, Jesus knew how to access the power. This kind of stuff only shifts when prayer, fasting and faith are brought to bear; and those commodities are not to do with your practice but your preparation.

The fact of the matter is that Jesus did not pray and fast before delivering the boy – not at the point of delivery anyway. His explanation points towards the long lonely hours on the hills with his Father. Allowing faith to build in hours of solitude, life-shaping prayer, Scripture-saturation and soul-shaping fasting, Jesus did not just know *what* to do, but also *how* to do it.

Disciples are not going to be formed by a focus on WWJD, unless there is a parallel challenge to ask HDJDI? In forming disciples, we therefore must give high priority not just to the outcome of a Jesus-following lifestyle but also to the inputs that are required to achieve such a lifestyle.

To do that, we need to devote ourselves to training in the basic disciplines of the Christian life, teaching ourselves and those we are accompanying as fellow-disciples to step out of the rush of (post?)modern life and immerse ourselves in the life-shaping presence of the Lord that we follow.

If we are to be evangelistic leaders in the mode of Jesus, creating cultures of outreach as Jesus did in his discipleship group and equipping grass-roots evangelistic leaders to empower every member for ministry, then we simply must focus on the HDJDI? question. We must stop confusing activity with spirituality and hurry with holiness, and invest in the things that ultimately will make our outreach effective.

9. Life-long learning

Discipleship is the ultimate life-long learning package. We never graduate (not until Jesus comes back anyway) and all of our lives are spent wearing the 'L plates' which mark us out as learners.

Every twist and turn of life brings new learning experiences to our discipleship programme. Poverty and wealth; youth and ageing; singleness, marriage – and even divorce; employment and unemployment; love and loneliness – you get the picture: every season of life demands that we learn from Jesus how to respond as though he were us.

This is a challenge for those of us who are leading. Often 'discipleship' is portrayed as a packaged course that we lead new converts through so that they have been 'discipled.' However, to see discipleship as life-long learning requires us to address the issue of how well we support life-long learners throughout the changing scenes of their lives.

Maybe there needs to be a mixed economy of learning support opportunities in our churches consisting of short-courses, discussion groups or sermon series which are run from time to time, giving disciples at different levels of maturity the tools to reflect on what Jesus requires of them, in regard to the issues that are arising in their lives.

Alongside these systematic structural life-support systems, there does need to be a personal life-support system which ensures that every disciple has someone who they can turn to and learn from at different times in their lives. This may of course happen through natural contact and friendships within the church, but it may also be the place where a church needs to examine its small group structures to ensure that there are not too many holes in the discipleship-support net (more on small groups in the next chapter).

10. *The disciple's life-support*

When I was a child, my parents started taking to me to church every Sunday. The morning service was fine because we had Sunday school but in the evening service there was no provision for we 'little ones' and so we had to find our own entertainment to survive the service (and especially the sermon).

I had two strategies, the first of which was to play out in my head what would happen if robbers burst in and took the collection bags off the communion table in the middle of the service (I always had the starring role: 007 eat your heart out). When I'd finished saving the Lord's £15 6s 9d, I turned to my second strategy, which was far less dramatic and consisted of counting the number of wooden planks which formed the wall cladding behind the pulpit.

I could never quite be certain whether there were 72 or 73 planks, partly because half-way across the wall (at around plank 36) my eye was distracted by a text that had been painted there.

'Lo! I am with you always, even unto the end of the world. Matt. XXVIII v. XX.'

At the time I had no idea what all the XXs and VIs were all about, and more significantly, I had no idea what wonderful truth the words themselves contained.

Now I know better (28:20 right?). Disciple-making and discipleship itself was not to be a hard slog following in the impossibly huge footsteps of Jesus but rather a journey on which he was my faithful travelling companion, walking with me and working in me to help me to do the discipleship thing.

The Greek words translated 'always' apparently literally means, 'the whole of every day' and that's a fantastic slant on the promise. Yes, discipleship is about a commitment to start anew, renouncing old masters and accepting Jesus' mastery of my life. Yes, it's about learning new things from him so that my whole life is reshaped around his will and word. Yes, it's about a life-long learning package on a course that I never graduate from. But it is not a *self*-improvement course; I do not walk this path alone. Jesus is with me 'the whole of every day'; encouraging, speaking, forgiving, correcting, directing and empowering.

The resurrection and ascension mean that Christian discipleship is not a determination to follow the dusty teachings of an historical guru; rather we live each day in the resurrection presence of Jesus, led by his Spirit into ever new discoveries of his grace and goodness.

Maybe one of the best ways that we can help one another as disciples is to learn together how to discern the presence of Jesus in 'the whole of every day.' At work and play; in the public and intimate moments of life; with friends and when alone: what does it mean that Jesus is with me?

From the one to the many

'Discipleship' then is a whole-life commitment to follow Jesus. Those of us wishing to be evangelistic leaders creating cultures of outreach in our churches have to first reflect on the health of our own discipleship and of the discipleship structures that we have in place in our churches. The questions below may be a helpful place to begin that reflection.

We've looked at the issue of disciple-making from several angles, but there remains one crucial issue which we have only touched on indirectly: the issue of the relationship that we as individual disciples have with one another. This is such an important area that it moves us on into the next dimension of what it means to be church – and into our next chapter.

Questions for leaders

1. *Discipleship not conversion*

- Which phrase is more frequently used in your church when referring to evangelism: making disciples or making converts?

- On a piece of paper draw two columns headed 'Making converts' and 'Making disciples.' What do you consider the main differences between the two activities?

2. *No discipleship: no outreach*

- Think of the people in your church who you consider to be grass-roots evangelists. Do they bear out the statement: no discipleship: no outreach?

- What do you do to maintain a passionate spirituality? How could you help other in your church do the same?

3. *Disciples are passionate lovers*

- How do you ensure that love for Jesus is always seen as the main thing in your church?

- How does our outreach make Jesus appear attractive in our neighbourhoods and networks?

4. *Make disciples ... baptizing them*

- When was the last time you issued an invitation for people in your church to be baptized? How about making one soon?

- Where do you think the challenge to repentance comes in the lives of those who have begun relating to Jesus?

5. *Make disciples ... teach them to obey*

- Review your discipleship teaching programmes. Do they prioritize spiritual things over issues of practical living?

- How do we encourage people to be doers and not just hearers of the word?

6. *Disciples need disciplers*

- Is the mentoring and teaching of disciples in your church more formal or informal? Are you happy with the balance?

- How do you respond to be an example of Christian living in the eyes of the flock?

7. *Disciples fail*

- What is your attitude towards people who fall on their discipleship journey? Are they failures or learners?

- What have you learned from your own failures in following Jesus that will make your ministry more compassionate towards others who fall?

8. *HDJDI? not just WWJD?*

- How do you keep your commitment to the spiritual disciplines at the forefront of your leadership?

- List everything that happens in the life of your church to encourage disciples to engage with the spiritual disciplines. What more could happen?

9. *Life-long learning*

- Think of three members of your church who represent different age-bands and/or different levels of Christian maturity. What do you think their needs are in terms of their discipleship? How is the church helping to meet those needs?

- How do you and the members of your leadership team maintain your own life-long learning as disciples of Jesus?

10. *The disciple's life-support*

- What has been your recent experience of Jesus being with you the whole of every day?

- How can we help people in the church discover the presence of Jesus in every moment of their lives?

Chapter 8

Forming Community

'The building of communities, fully a part of their localities yet radically distinct, is a priority in [Christian] mission.'

Stuart Murray[1]

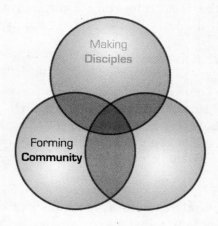

In Part One Philip talked about the need to shift from a view of outreach as being principally about activities that we do, to one of being a culture which we embrace. The idea of a culture simply expresses that 'different groups

---

[1] Stuart Murray, *The Challenge of the City: A Biblical View* (Tonbridge: Sovereign World, 1993), p. 101.

of people have different ways of life.'[2] So what are the distinctive marks of the 'way of life' embraced by groups of disciples of Jesus Christ? What kinds of 'ways of life' form the *context* for the creation of a culture of outreach?

Chief amongst the 'proofs' of discipleship that Jesus offered us was that authentic discipleship would be evidenced in the quality of our relationships with other disciples.

Love lessons

When Jesus was concerned to present the essence of essential discipleship he pointed towards relationships as the key.

'What's the most important commandment, Jesus?' Which of all the laws that keep God happy, keeps him happiest?

Mmm. What to choose?

> "Love the Lord your God with all your passion and prayer and intelligence." This is the most important, the first on any list. But there is a second to set alongside it: "Love others as well as you love yourself." These two commands are pegs; everything in God's Law and the Prophets hangs from them.[3]

Interesting that Jesus simply could not answer the question by selecting just one commandment. Of course, the command to put God first, to yield to him heart, soul, mind and strength, had to come top, but what if his

---

[2] Gareth Morgan, *Images of Organization* (Thousand Oaks, CA: SAGE Publications, 1997), p. 120.

[3] Matthew 22 – Eugene Peterson, *The Message: The Bible in Contemporary Language* (Colorado Springs, CO: NavPress, 2002), p. 1790.

hearers should imagine that they could somehow love God without expressing that in their relationships with one another? The fact that Jesus just had to keep God-love and other-love welded together in the top-spot should alert us to the importance of relationships in God's outreach programme.

Some time later, Jesus is sharing his final meal with his disciples when events take an unexpected and slightly embarrassing turn. He starts to undress. Then, as the disciples look from one to the other to see what would happen next, he pulls on an apron, fills a bowl with water and begins to wash their dirty feet.

One by one before their amazed eyes he painstakingly and lovingly works his way around the group, seeming to pause for a moment before taking Judas' feet in his hands, but carrying on to wash them anyway.

Conversation is difficult with Jesus acting so oddly. Peter tries to bluff his way out of his embarrassment but Jesus is having none of it.

'What's going on, Jesus?'

'Well, you call me your Master and Lord, right?' Twelve heads nod; so far so good.

'And that means that you want to learn from me about life, the universe and everything, right?' More nods.

'So now I've washed your feet, not because you're dirty but because you're a bit slow. This is to teach you a lesson that you otherwise may not get. I've laid down a pattern for you. What I've done, you do. I'm only pointing out the obvious ... If you understand what I'm telling you, act like it – and live a blessed life.'

You'd have thought that was plain enough. The God-blessed life comes through practising servant-style love for one another. But just in case their thick Galilean heads still hadn't got it, Jesus can't resist a second stab at getting this most crucial missional message across.

'Let me give you a new command: Love one another. In the same way I loved you, you love one another.' This is really important, the acid test of whether or not you really are following him. In fact 'this is how everyone will recognize that you are my disciples – when they see the love you have for each other.'[4]

So that's it: our second arena of authentic Jesus-centred church is defined for us by the Master himself. Not content to draw people to himself in radical life-reshaping loving commitment (or discipleship, to give it its shorter name) Jesus brings the second movement alongside it: love one another. Just as when he had answered the Pharisees he had been unable to disengage the practice of loving those around us from a profession of love for God, so here in his final hours he urgently presses the truth home through dramatic action, direct commandment and extravagant example; *loving one another is crucial to your mission as my followers.*

Whether we are evangelistic leaders, grass-roots leaders or every-member missionaries, the quality of our relationships with one another will always be integral to our ability to make Jesus known to the watching world.

Body talk

To be on mission in the Jesus way is therefore not firstly about what we do 'in the world' but how we live 'in the church.' Understanding what loving one another 'as Jesus has loved us' looks like is the primary work of being church together (apparently).

Now some will be twitching nervously at this point and worrying that this is beginning to sound like an excuse

---

4 John 13 – Eugene Peterson, *The Message: The Bible in Contemporary Language* (Colorado Springs, CO: NavPress, 2002), p. 1949.

for an evangelical love-in and nothing to do with creating a culture of outreach in a missional church; but it's not. In fact, learning to love lavishly in the church is the prelude to learning to love lavishly in the world, and it is this love that is itself profoundly missional because it is the heartbeat of the kind of deeply attractive community which Philip talked about in chapter 5.

'The church must *first of all* reflect and represent the Lordship of Christ *in itself.*'[5] It cannot export what it doesn't have; unless it has learned to be a community where divisions of race, gender and wealth (to mention just three barriers) have fallen, where the poor receive good news, the lonely find family-style warmth and the broken are helped to reconnect their lives, how can it reach out in love to a divided, lonely and broken world?

Lesslie Newbigin, missionary and missiologist observed, on returning to the UK from years on the mission field in India, that the missionary task facing the UK church was at least as big, possibly bigger, than that facing the churches in India where he had served for so long. He recognized that for people in the West to understand the gospel, it could not be reduced to a few alphabeticalized propositional truths (the ABCD of salvation): it had to be embodied, partly for pragmatic reasons – that was what would work – and partly for theological reasons – that was the way Jesus did it.

'Jesus did not write a book but formed a community' observed Newbigin, 'a community that exists in him and for him.' The life of this community should be the most eloquent testimony to a healing God of love, who heals through a cross.

---

[5] Jürgen Moltmann, *The Church in the Power of the Spirit* (London: SCM Press, 1992[2]), p. 106, emphasis added.

Everything suggests that it is absurd to believe that the true authority over all things is represented in a crucified man. No amount of argument can make it sound reasonable ... [and] that is why I am suggesting that the only possible hermeneutic of the gospel is a congregation which believes it.[6]

Newbigin's suggestion points to the missional significance of Jesus' new commandment. A community that is learning to love as it has been loved, and which embraces others in that love, will be deeply attractive. Building individual disciples into authentic communities, far from being a distraction from mission, is therefore crucial to creating cultures of outreach.

Family first

It is important to note that the discipleship community is a family, not a foundation; it's about relationships, not rituals and about sharing life together, not just singing songs together. Yes, we do need to organize ourselves (more of that in the next chapter) but the organization is there to serve a purpose: to enhance our relationships with God (discipleship), with one another (forming community) and ultimately with the world of the non-churched (touching society). When the organizational structures demand higher allegiance than the purpose for which they were created, you know you've got problems.

This is an especially hard but important lesson for church leaders who frequently face the temptation to imagine that their job is about getting people to participate in church structures. 'Discipleship' then gets unhelpfully

---

6 Lesslie Newbigin, *The Gospel in a Pluralist Society* (London: SPCK, 1989), p. 227, 232.

melded with 'church membership' and is measured not by degrees of transformation to be more like Jesus, but by degrees of perspiration offered in ever deeper commitment to church activities. Keeping the church show on the road is only important if the road is clearly leading towards Jesus and his concern for the lost.

Evangelistic leaders, on the other hand, know that the structural 'wine skins' of church life are endlessly flexible because they are there for one thing only: to keep the wine fresh so that when it is poured out into the world, it tastes great!

I want to suggest three distinctives that we can expect to see in a church that understands its *relationships* (and not its structures, buildings or meetings) to be the very essence of its nature and purpose. They are: sacrificial love, Spirit-empowered service and stimulating worship.

1. Sacrificial love

In John 13 Jesus raised the stakes of his observation (recorded in Matthew) that the greatest thing we humans could do was to love God and love one another 'as much as we love ourselves.' That sounds a tall order, but in John we read that Jesus challenged his disciples to a higher love: love 'as he has loved us.'

As-he-has-loved-us love is surely about a depth of commitment that goes beyond cosy niceties to cruel nails, beyond tea and buns to a towel and bowl full of smelly feet. Love in the Christian community is not expressed by pleasantries, warm smiles and hugging at Hallelujah parties (though personally I'm in favour of all three) but rather As-he-has-loved-us love requires that I purposely enter into a depth of commitment to you that means even when you are at your worst, I will still give you my best.

As-he-has-loved-us love is a decision that leads to an action: something like 'God so loved the world that he gave', sums up as-he-has-loved-us love. Or how about, 'God put his love on the line for us by offering his Son in a sacrificial death while we were no use whatever to him.'[7]

The first Christians understood this and took it literally. Sociologist and historian Rodney Stark states that whilst this kind of behaviour was 'alien to paganism' in the first two centuries, Christians fully understood that

> because God loves humanity, Christians cannot please God unless they *love one another*. Indeed as God demonstrates his love through sacrifice, humans must demonstrate their love through sacrifice on behalf of *one another*.[8]

To illustrate his point Stark goes on to tell the stories of the ways that Christians' responses to the major plague epidemics that hit the world at that time were at variance with the responses of the surrounding pagans. The basic pagan's response was to run away and hope to save their lives: the basic Christian's response was to stay put and hope to save someone else's life. Indeed so successful were they at looking after one another (and their non-believing neighbours) that their survival rates were markedly higher than those of the world around, leaving the church proportionally stronger in society after the plagues than before them – even though many Christians did succumb to the disease and die.

But what might it look like in a contemporary church if people started exercising As-he-has-loved-us love (assuming the absence of plagues)?

We're reluctant to offer a list because we don't want to appear to be suggesting a new legalism, but if love is about

---

[7] Romans 5 – Eugene Peterson, *The Message: The Bible in Contemporary Language* (Colorado Springs, CO: NavPress, 2002).

[8] Rodney Stark, *The Rise of Christianity* (San Francisco: HarperCollins, 1997), p. 86.

sacrifice on behalf of another (and it is in New Testament terms) then you can start working out for yourself what it would mean for me to subjugate my assumed 'rights' to my Christian 'responsibilities.'

> My assumed 'right' to be treated fairly is sacrificed in favour of my responsibility to forgive you, so I overlook your misrepresentation of my behaviour and refuse to bear you a grudge.

> My assumed 'right' to spend the money I've earned on myself is sacrificed in favour of my responsibility to share what I have with you, so I forego the iPod accessory and offer to help meet your pressing need instead.

> My assumed 'right' to set my own agenda for my life is willingly sacrificed in favour of my responsibility to react to your need for a listening ear, so I give you the time I'd set aside to watch the football (is there a greater sacrifice?)

As-he-has-loved-us communities are constructed of hundreds of small behind-the-scenes building blocks which slowly but surely create a counter-culture where 'other' takes precedence of 'self.' This is a huge challenge in our individualistic, fragmented society, but we really believe that there is no alternative if we are to create healthy, healing missional communities.

When we create our training programmes for would-be evangelistic leaders, I would make sure that understanding 'As-he-has-loved-us love' was high on the list of topics to be covered. It is impossible to embed a Culture of Outreach in a non-loving environment, so let's think a little more about how to go about creating one.

Small groups   As-he-has-loved-us kinds of churches will only happen when people build relationships together that are sufficiently open and honest that their needs are shared. You've got to be close to someone to wash their feet.

Inevitably, this will mean that church life must be organized around some kind of small group system, in which people meet regularly to share their lives and serve one another.

Church health gurus tell us that small groups are a key to healthy church; but not just any sort of small group will do. The healthiest kind of small group experience is one in which people see their group not as another midweek meeting, but where they understand it as a network of relationships – a family within the wider church family – which is there, throughout every day of every week, and where 'one another' love is worked out.

The New Testament is crammed with injunctions to look out for one another. We 'belong to one another' so we should 'love one another', 'pray for one another', 'care for one another', 'serve one another', 'forgive one another', 'teach one another', 'encourage one another', 'show hospitality to one another', 'comfort one another' and even 'confess our faults to one another' and 'admonish one another.'[9]

All of this 'one another' activity does not naturally flow out of the often time-squeezed and shallow relational experience of a Sunday meeting. Nor, for many, will it 'just happen' in the context of close Christian friendships: too many people do not have such things.

If the Sunday (or Saturday or whatever) experience has little community-building potential and the coverage of natural friendships is, at best, patchy, there are two

---

[9] Romans 12:5; 1 John 3:11; James 5:16; 1 Corinthians 12:25,26; Galatians 5:13; Ephesians 4:32; Colossians 3:16; Hebrews 3:13; 1 Peter 4:9.

contrasting ways in which churches seek to respond to the imperative to form caring communities.

One is to employ a professional carer; let's call them 'Vicar' or 'Pastor.' Having appointed them, let's breathe a sigh of relief and get on with our day jobs, leaving them to care for us. After a year, having watched them burn themselves out, let's bewail the fact that we haven't been visited for six months and suggest they look for employment elsewhere because they are not suited to the ministry. Sound familiar?

The other way is to agree to commit ourselves to As-he-has-loved-us love by caring and supporting *one another* within our church small group family. After all, Sundays are too rushed, friendships are too patchy and professional care is too scarce a resource.

I could tell you many stories of where this kind of love has been shared within the Christian community – and where it has overflowed into those outside: the non-Christian husband of a church member who was bowled over by God's love as he witnessed the way the church cared for his wife during her convalescence following major surgery. Or I could mention the middle-aged woman who just turned up on the doorstep of a church leader asking about 'his God' after church members had devoted time, energy and money to replacing the flood-damaged carpets of her elderly mother.

'In *The Finding Faith Today* research more than 80 per cent of those who had come to faith said that the main factor in bringing them to faith was a relationship. Interestingly, only a quarter of these people said that it was a friendship with just one person: for most it was a friendship with a group of people ...'[10] Small groups with

---

[10] John Finney, *Emerging Evangelism* (London: Darton, Longman & Todd, 2004), p. 136.

a developing culture of outreach are therefore especially well-placed to reach out to neighbours and networks with the kind of practical, sacrificial love that they have practised at home.

Living as Jesus' disciples under the shadow of the cross demands that we embrace the cross as the distinctive pattern for our lives within the Christian community – and as we do so, our missional impact is enhanced as well. However, in case this all sounds a bit too much like hard work, we need to move on to our second distinctive of authentic Christian community – the presence and work of the Holy Spirit.

2. *Spirit-empowered service*

Helen rang me, her voice betraying that something exciting had happened. The week previously her best friend Jane had come to faith in Jesus at the end of our Sunday meeting. Helen had been keeping in touch and had just had a phone call from Jane who had been quite surprised by something she'd just experienced.

Apparently she'd been having a bath whilst listening to a Christian worship CD that Helen had loaned her. As she soaked and listened she suddenly found herself joining in – but in a language she didn't recognize. It was a bit of shock, to put it mildly, and she ran from the bathroom to phone Helen to ask what on earth was going on.

Helen had to explain that sometimes God graciously provides a new language for his children to pray and praise with, and that Jane had just received that wonderful gift. This was the first time Jane had heard of such a thing but Helen's careful counsel at that point put her mind at rest and released her from any fear about using that gift in the future.

Thank God that there is more to church than a bunch of enthusiastic hard-working disciples. The first disciples were warned not to attempt missional activity until they received the Holy Spirit,[11] and we would do well to heed the same warning.

The empowering presence of the Holy Spirit, taking up residence in Jesus' disciples and the communities they create, is actually what makes church 'church.' As Gordon Fee explains, 'The people of God as a community of believers owe their existence to their common, lavish experience of the Spirit.'[12] But how does this work of the Spirit make an impact on the creation of Christian community and in the forming of cultures of outreach within them?

Whilst the work of the Spirit is individual and unpredictable (unpredictable in that, in my experience, no two people experience his work in exactly the same way) the impact of that individual experience has a natural outworking in the life of the Christian community.

Just as 'love' has to be a reality in the Christian community before it can be exported to the world, so the work and life of the Spirit is first an internal reality, which then proceeds to impact the world.

Paul gives us our best insights here, with his richly descriptive image of the church as the body of Jesus. Jesus is the head – the source of life and brains of the outfit. We are each and everyone charged with being the steward of some vital ingredient of the body's life, *for the good of the body*. Therefore, the degree to which we understand our bodily function (if you pardon the phrase) and live out our Spirit-inspired vocation will determine the health of the body.

For churches to be healthy and equipped to reach the world around them, it is vital that every individual

---

[11] Acts 1:4f.

[12] Gordon Fee, *God's Empowering Presence: The Holy Spirit in the Letters of Paul* (Carlisle: Paternoster, 1994), p. 872.

member of the church is encouraged to see what form the Spirit's motivation within them is taking. Every-member-missionaries may express their missionary calling in all manner of ways, as the Spirit equips and leads, and once discovered, this Spirit-given urge creates a mandate for serving which is hard to repress.

How that is done will vary. Personally, I'm not a great fan of these multiple-choice 'tick-a-box-and-win-a-ministry' type of exercises. We recently completed one in my church homegroup and I scored '0' for the gift of mercy. Now given that I've spent most of my life in pastoral ministry, I was more than a little perturbed by the finding that I have absolutely no capacity to show mercy to people.

The feeling of disappointment was not helped when I went home and told my wife that I had scored *zero* points in the mercy gift column, and she simply looked at me with her 'how-am-I-going-to-do-this without-offending-him' look, shrugged her shoulders and said, 'Well?'

It wasn't the affirmation that I wanted so I went back to the questionnaire and filtered out the questions that allegedly proved that I was running on empty in the mercy department. The author of the questionnaire had apparently decided that 'merciful' people are identified by the fact that they just love visiting people in hospital and elderly people's homes. The questions identifying the 'mercy' gift all went something like:

'I gain deep joy by giving my time to visit the sick in hospital' – Always? Usually? Sometimes? Never?

Answer? *Never,* never, never do I even get close to ordinary joy – never mind deep joy (whatever that is) – from visiting people in hospital. I hate the places but does that mean that I have no mercy?

So if there are shortcomings in the questionnaire approach to gift discovery, how do we help people release that which God has placed within them, for the good of the church? People need *instruction*, opportunity for *reflection* and guided *application*.

Instruction   The first step to helping people consider how God has gifted them to serve his purposes is to open up what the Bible has to say about the nature and purpose of spiritual gifts.

My favourite starting place is actually in a verse which doesn't explicitly mention gifts, Philippians 2:13, which tells us that 'God is always at work in [us] to make us willing and able to obey his own purpose.'[13] The spiritual gifts that God gives to each individual are there to realign our life-purpose with God's, and to equip us with the particular abilities required to achieve them.

People need to understand that since God's purposes embrace all of life (ultimately the reconciliation of all things to himself) so our gifts have a 'whole-life' orientation too. It would therefore be wrong to imagine that the real 'spiritual gifts' are supernatural (tongues, healing, prophesying) and the ordinary gifts listed in the Bible (being a craftsman, showing hospitality etc) are somehow 'second class gifts.' *All* the gifts are supernatural if they arise from the impulse of God's Spirit making us 'willing and able' to work with God towards achieving his purposes.

Having made sure that people understand the nature of purpose of spiritual gifts in Scripture, I have found that most people naturally gravitate towards a ministry or occupation that makes sense of their gifts (the questionnaires simply affirm what they already know).

Reflection   However, where someone seeks help to discover or affirm their gifting, I have found that it can be helpful

---

[13]   Good News Bible.

to work through a list of discussion questions with them.[14] The questions that I use are included at Appendix 4. I first came across the idea for the list a few years ago and have subsequently expanded it a bit.

No single question on the list defines a person's gift, but in discussion with a mature Christian something will begin to emerge that points towards what God has equipped and motivated that person to contribute to the health of the local body – and the wider world.

Application   Finally, there needs to be some help given in using one's gifts appropriately. This will involve finding appropriate avenues of service – within the church or beyond – where the gifts that God has placed within a person by his Spirit can make the biggest possible impact for the purposes of the kingdom of God.

If the service opportunity is in the church, the church leader needs to ensure that the ministry is as well supported as possible, with ministry guidelines prepared beforehand so that everyone is clear about what is being asked or offered and with agreed dates for meetings with ministry team leaders or line-managers for regular review. Embedding all ministries within good and clearly defined support structures is crucial for the effective health of that ministry.

However, in some research that I carried out I discovered that fitting someone's ministry to their gifting was the single most important factor in keeping them motivated in their work. This means that church leaders may need to start with the worker rather than the work, when devising the shape of church activities. Rather than saying (for example), 'These are the strands of our evangelism

---

14   I first came across the bare bones of this approach on a taped set of teaching by Greg Haslam, then of Winchester City Church.

strategy for the next year' and trying to recruit people into that predefined shape, a person-centred (or 'gift-centred') approach will ask, 'How can the gifts and interests of the people in the church be used to provide creative contact points with our friends and neighbours?'

If the evangelism strategy is built around the gifts of the people in the church – and directed at the needs of the people in the community – my research indicates that the workers will be more engaged and fulfilled, meaning that people in the community will receive a more attractive point of contact with the church.

For example, Sandra was one of the most fruitful evangelists in our church. She was a businesswoman who ran a successful beauty salon. In the context of her work – which she (mostly) loved – she met loads of people who would never think of coming to a church service and who would probably hesitate to even come to a social gathering organized by Christians. They did, however, trust Sandra and value the service she offered (no pun intended) at her salon.

We could have tried to get Sandra to join the team of one of our church outreach activities and use her people skills there, but Sandra hit on the great idea of running events actually within her business where she was gifted, trusted and spent most of her time anyway. So we worked with Sandra to run 'stress-relief' courses, fashion evenings and eventually Alpha courses for her customers – and guess what – they attended!

Working with Sandra where she was already gifted and committed was much more fruitful than taking her out of that environment and placing her into a 'church' role where she was operating to our agenda rather than her own.

Have a look around your church. Are there outreach activities that are a constant struggle to staff? A general rule of thumb is that if you have to start scratching around asking 'Who can we get to run X?' then it may well be time to scrap X all together and look first at what gifts your people are bringing to the kingdom party.

Implicit in all of this is that the presence of the Spirit – God's empowering presence – is what makes the difference between church and any other organization. We need to seek him, cherish him, celebrate him and serve one another with the gifts that each of us have received from him. This challenge to help those who belong to our churches to discover, treasure, hone and use their gifts – in all of life, including the church – is central to the formation of Christian community and thus central to the work of evangelistic leadership.

Let's move now to the third aspect of forming the kind of authentic Christian community that is fit enough to engage with a lost and hurting world.

3. *Stimulating Worship*

'The church is first of all an *assembly*: "where two or three are *gathered* in my name, I am there among them".'[15] In other words, gathering together for service and worship is part of the discipline of life that marks us out as church.

Gathering around the presence of the living Jesus, in large or small groups, is surely intended to be one of the high points of Christian experience: encountering the One who loves to loiter among the lampstands of his church.[16] Gathering with the expectancy that Jesus is going to be present is, however, surprisingly challenging. Research indicates that increasing numbers of Christians are taking

---

[15] Miroslav Wolf, *After Our Likeness: The Church As the Image of the Trinity* (Grand Rapids, MI: Eerdmans, 1998), p. 137, his emphasis.

[16] See Revelation 1:12.

the option of meeting Jesus in this way on average just twice a month, with mini-breaks, visits to distant family, golf and even shopping trips being reckoned to be of greater importance.

How do we respond as church leaders? Commonly, if I'm honest, my response was marked by resentment and jealousy: resentment that they hadn't come to play today and jealousy that I myself didn't have the freedom to choose the beach rather than the preach.

Could it be, however, that maybe – just maybe – the responsibility for the loss of commitment to gather frequently with Jesus' family lies with *our* meetings rather than *their* choices? If people really were sensing the presence of the living Lord Jesus in our meetings, would they seriously choose the shopping mall instead?

The challenge is to make sure that our gatherings centre on Jesus the incarnate, crucified, risen, ascended and returning Lord of Life. They must be about the re-orientation of our lives in the presence of the living Lord and Saviour of the cosmos. Research has indicated that worship which leads people into the presence of God is vital to the missional health of the church and to the spiritual health of the individual disciples that constitute the church.[17] This is not linked to any particular style of worship, but rather to the ability of that style to enable people to encounter the presence of God; it may be charismatic enthusiasm for some or cathedral elegance for others.

Our experience has also shown that stimulating worship has a positive impact on guests attending our churches. I can think of many examples of people who

---

[17] Christian Schwarz, *Natural Church Development Handbook* (Moggerhanger: BCGA), pp. 30–31.

over the years have got hooked on worship before they ever came to faith in Jesus.

Neil, now my home group leader, was an avid Sunday morning golfer who attended church at his wife's request and never made it back to the greens; Jason, the head-teacher of a local school, came along after starting to attend an Alpha course and has hardly missed a Sunday since. Simon, living apart from his wife after an affair, attended at the request of his son who was in our youth work and was strongly drawn by his sense of God speaking to him in our services (it's a good story; he came to faith, was reconciled to his wife and is now an elder in the church).

The point of all this is that whilst it is rare (though still not unknown) for people to wander in off the streets, when our members do pluck up the courage and bring friends along to a meeting – whether it's a special guest service or just a 'normal' Sunday service – we can expect the God who centres himself in the praises of his people to exert his drawing power. We just need to make sure that we don't get in the way and look at the way we plan and lead our services to make sure that people encounter God and not a dodgy drama, unintelligible talk or poorly led praise.

We'll be thinking more about how to strategically place guest services in our programmes in the last chapter but for now let's think a little more about the elements of healthy God-revealing gatherings.

Celebrating the presence   Robert Warren suggests that there are several ways in which church services can 'energize the faith' of those participating. His sugges-tions include the use of *silence* (a scarce commodity in today's world), the use of *testimonies and stories*, 'in which people share experiences of God's actions', and a deliberately focused *celebration* of the 'reality and goodness of God.'[18]

The one act perhaps above all other in which Jesus continues to offer himself to us is in the *bread and wine of communion*. The presence of the bread and wine reminds us that our worship is rooted in something other than ourselves and our ability to 'get it right.' We do not have to create something by our attempts to worship but rather recognize the presence of someone. The worry that I may not be good enough (as a singer, dancer, pray-er, etc) is corrected by the bread and wine which assures me that I am accepted not because of my ability to sing, but because of Jesus' ability to sacrifice himself on my behalf.

Another crucial element of our gatherings must surely be faith-filled *prayer*. As a church leader I remember being confused and somewhat disappointed when I tried to suggest that we spend more time in our Sunday meetings praying for one another. The response I received was 'But just imagine if we get visitors in.' So I did and I reckoned that the average visitor probably wouldn't be too shocked if they found people in a church meeting praying. Indeed, given that prayer is a universal language (surveys often show that more people pray than either claim to have faith or believe in a god – work that one out) it should be seeker-friendly.

It is ironic that at the time when society is open to the language and experience of spirituality that the church is 'demystifying' itself in order to be seeker-friendly. *Q* magazine, commenting on the work of John Taverner, composer and member of the Orthodox Church wrote,

---

[18] Robert Warren, *The Healthy Churches Handbook: a process for revitalizing your church* (London: Church House Publishing, 2004), p. 20.

'Christianity's talent for shooting itself in the foot is nowhere better displayed than in its recent drive to demystify itself. After all, who goes to church to get reasonable? Mystery is precisely what used to draw the crowds; no wonder the gates are down.'[19]

Finally, it would be an oversight were we not to mention the place of the Bible in the spectrum of activities that make God's presence real to us in our gatherings. There are certainly challenges to be faced in presenting Scripture as a living life-giving resource in today's culture, however. Scripture itself is what keeps us on track with engaging with God's mission in God's way. As Stuart Murray observes, 'hearing substantial portions of the biblical text read aloud regularly, with or without exposition, earths the community in the story of God's mission, within which it finds its own identity and destiny.'[20]

Preaching, at best, when performed by gifted people is that gift which examines, explains and embeds God's word in the hearts of his people so that (as Roger Forster of Ichthus puts it) their 'blood becomes *bibline*' and their every thought, desire and deed is being taken captive by Jesus and for Jesus.

Summary

So how are we doing? Pursuing our main thought, that the first priority of Jesus' disciples is to form communities in which the life of Jesus is expressed in 'as-he-has-loved-us' relationships, we have noted the core distinctives of such a group as being

---

[19] Quoted in John Finney, *Emerging Evangelism* (London: Darton, Longman & Todd, 2004), p. 31.

[20] Stuart Murray, *Church After Christendom* (Bletchley: Paternoster, 2004), p. 211.

- Sacrificial relationships
- Spirit-empowered service
- Stimulating worship

Any church that wants to create a culture of outreach and develop 'winning ways' has to look within itself to address these three core issues of church health. We all want to see new 'spiritual babies' being born but surely God is disinclined to add his newly adopted children to a family that is at war with itself, full of jaded cynics whose chief occupation is having the pastor for Sunday lunch.

Like any responsible parent, God wants to place his newborn children in a safe and welcoming environment, where people love him and love one another, where they use their Spirit-given gifts to serve one another, where they will be stimulated to know and love him more by their experience of his presence in times of gathered worship.

Idealistic? Maybe – but we believe this vision of church-as-community is God's platform for launching us out to touch society in his lost world. It is to this third dimension of church-as-Jesus intended that we now turn in our final chapter.

Questions for leaders

1. *Sacrificial love*

- What evidence do you see in your church that the people in it are ready to lay down their lives for one another?

- If somebody in your church had an urgent need, how would they communicate that within the church family?

2. *Spirit-empowered service*

• At what stage in their relationship with your church are people encouraged to identify and use their gifts to serve one another?

• What do you understand the greater gifts of 1 Corinthians 14:1 to be? How are they sought in your church?

3. *Stimulating worship*

• Ask around and find out which elements of your gatherings really help people to feel that they have encountered God. What do you make of your findings?

• Ask the most recent newcomers to your church (ideally people with little or no Christian background) what they felt like when they first attended one of your services? What most impressed them and what most confused them?

Chapter 9

Touching Society

'Our missionary activities are only authentic insofar as they reflect participation in the mission of God.'

David Bosch[1]

'I have come to seek and to save the lost.'

Jesus Christ[2]

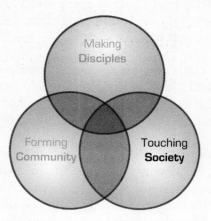

What we have been trying to state thus far in Part 2 is that the mission of the church *has* to be expressed in the

---

[1] David J. Bosch, *Transforming Mission: Paradigm Shifts in Theology of Mission* (New York: Orbis, 1991), p. 391.

[2] Luke 19:10.

way that the mission of Jesus was: by calling disciples who form communities that touch society. Often 'mission' is portrayed as being just the third of those distinctives – activities which aim at touching society – but Jesus-shaped mission must contain all three distinctives since each requires the other to be present if it is to 'work':

- You cannot form Christian communities unless you have disciples of Jesus to start with.

- You cannot make disciples in the first place unless in some way you are touching society (where else would they come from?)

- You cannot nurture those disciples unless you have healthy communities (see previous chapter).

- A crucial part of developing individual disciples is envisioning and equipping them as they engage with everyday life in society.

Thus every 'circle' of our diagram overlaps with every other circle and must continue to do so. In fact, we believe that one of the most important tasks for church leaders is to ensure that all three circles are in healthy balance in church life.

With all of this talk about discipleship and Christian community, however, we have not forgotten that the main goal in this book is to equip church leaders with the perspectives and tools to become *essential evangelistic leaders*, like Timothy in Ephesus 'doing the work of an evangelist', by forming a culture of outreach within their churches. In this final chapter, therefore, we want to focus on the third area fundamental to church health, and outline the essential elements of healthy *outreach*.

Again, we are not saying that all of the mission of God is expressed in seeking and saving the lost, but we are saying that the mission of God is never less than that, even if at times it is more than that – reconciling the cosmos for example (Col. 1:19, 20).

In this chapter we will fairly briefly outline some of the key elements of being engaged with God's world (since much of that was covered in Part One) before moving on to ask how evangelistic leaders can join up the various pieces of their strategic planning so that outreach becomes the natural and continuing overflow of discipleship and community.

WWJD?

Jesus embodied God's mission to the world, which is to say that he showed us what God was concerned about and how he proposed to go about remedying it. Having showed us he left us, his disciples, with the mandate to continue that embodiment as his earth-bound body, now directed by its heaven-seated Lord.

Earlier we noted the fact that the church only has validity and the right to call itself 'Christian' in so far as it is perpetuating the life, values and ministry of Jesus of Nazareth. We can make exactly the same observation about the church's outreach: it is only valid if it is profoundly Jesus-centred in its goals and values.

So how did Jesus go about it? It seems to us that his mission to the world started in prayer (intercession), engaged with people where they were (incarnation), welcomed people and taught them (integration and information), challenged them to receive the kingdom (inspiration) and formed them into discipleship communities (initiation).

Let's think briefly about each of those facets of Jesus-shaped outreach.

1. *Intercession*

Prayer is a mystery that requires mastery for effective ministry.

We emphasized in chapter 3 that salvation is ultimately God's work. Only God can change hearts by a supernatural Spirit-to-spirit transaction. Mysterious though it is, however, we are not uninvolved in that spiritual work: we have been given spiritual tools to use and prayer is the sharpest in the box. We all know that, but just how many times does the *urgency* of getting the job done rob us of the *intimacy* of seeking God's guidance and blessing on the work.

For Jesus himself, intimacy with his Father in times of solitary prayerfulness was both a regular practice (Lk. 5:16) and a feature of his preparation for major turning points in his mission;[3] indeed his practice of seeking solitude is perhaps 'one of the most significant things that we can learn about his prayer life' – and also about his approach to mission.[4]

In honing each step of his engagement with the world in careful prayerfulness, Jesus ensured that his mission was shaped by 'the will of the one who sent' (Jn. 6:38) him and demonstrated that earnest prayerfulness is the essential first step towards effective Christian outreach. *But prayer is not just vital before we start reaching out: prayer needs to be both the first step and the accompaniment to every other step along the journey of reaching out with God's good news.*

Shaping creative and meaningful patterns of inter-cessory prayer is thus the first leadership challenge when

---

[3] E.g. before calling the disciples (Lk. 6:12), the transfiguration (Lk. 9:28) and the cross (Mt. 26:36).

[4] Sister Margaret Magdalen, *Jesus: Man of Prayer* (London: Hodder & Stoughton, 1987), p. 39.

shaping a church's outreach strategy. Do all groups in your church (including the leadership team) pray regularly for the lost? Is there prayer for neighbourhoods and networks in main services? Does every community outreach group (e.g. Mums and Tots; youth club) spend time praying for evangelistic fruitfulness in their work? If not, then here's the place to start changing things.

2. Incarnation

People bring people – relationships are the key. This was one of the key principles of outreach which we developed in chapter 2.

Josef is one of my best friends. I first met him when he started up as a self-employed car mechanic, and I took my car to him to be fixed. He was friendly, reliable and did a good job at reasonable rates (what more do you want from a car mechanic?) so I introduced a few other of my Christian friends to him. Gradually different ones shared their faith with Josef and it stirred a latent spiritual thirst within him which led to him developing a faith of his own.

I am absolutely certain that Josef would never have gone to a church meeting to hear about Jesus – he hates social occasions and crowds – but there in his workshop he was very open to discussing issues relating to Christianity. The bridge between Jesus and Josef was created by on-the-spot friendship, shared on Josef's home-turf.

This was, after all, how Jesus did it.

Personal relationships   In Jesus, the God of everyone and everywhere became someone and arrived somewhere so that we might know him: God, in Eugene Peterson's memorable phrase, 'moved into the neighborhood.'[5]

---

[5]   Eugene Peterson, *The Message: The Bible in Contemporary Language* (Colorado Springs, CO: NavPress, 2002), p. 1916.

'Whenever the church has made significant impact in mission, it has clothed the gospel in a way which resonates with the concerns, needs and aspirations of the surrounding community':[6] it talks their language and scratches where they itch.

It follows then that, hard on the heels of intercession, the number and nature of our connections with those outside of the church is the second key factor in fruitful evangelism. We've said it before but it is so important that we can't say it loudly enough, or often enough: prayer and personal contacts; intercession and incarnation; imploring the Father and impacting our friends, petitioning and partying ...

You can carry on the word games, but you get the point. The dynamic of effective prayer and the power of loving, serving relationships, constitute the most vital elements by far of any church's outreach.

- *Prayer* is the connection between heaven's resources and earth's needs; if you neglect it, you negate effective outreach

- *Making real connections* in the world of our friends and neighbours is the effective 'glue' that ultimately draws people to Jesus

In the first centuries of Christian mission 'it was friendship that was the most common way for individuals to approach the seemingly unapproachable Christian churches'[7] and nothing has changed into the twenty-first century.

---

[6] Robert Warren, *Building Missionary Congregations* (Church House Publishing, 1995), p. 21.

[7] Alan Kreider, *Worship and Evangelism in Pre-Christendom* (Cambridge: Grove Books, 1995), p. 17.

To create a healthy culture of outreach in our churches we have to work hard at getting this point across. We need our members to understand that individually we 'do church' in the worlds of family, work and friendships, and we as leaders need to be committed to this belief so that we are willing to release people's time for meaningful engagement in the world by placing limits on their involvement in 'church work.'

Helping our members see the connections they already make in their day-to-day lives as fertile ground for Christian outreach is a major challenge. One Anglican church in Bristol has a large notice above the door which everyone leaving a service cannot fail to notice. 'You are now entering your mission field' it reads. Exactly.

Presence in community   However, it is not just as individuals that the church touches society. Sometimes we organize ourselves corporately in social outreach programmes such as youth drop-in clubs, parent and toddlers groups, neighbourhood clear-up projects or student cafes (to cite just a few examples).

Sometimes churches run these projects as expressions of God's love for their communities: sometimes with the expectation – or at least hope – of seeing people come to faith.

Here again, though, it is not the quality of the project which principally attracts people to Jesus (though it may stir initial interest in the church); what counts in these projects is the presence of Christian people whose love for Jesus overflows into the lives of those non-believers who are met. Again, relationships are the key.

If the quality of our relationships is a key to winning people to Jesus, then evangelistic church leaders will want to ask how well their churches prepare their individual members to develop what Brian McLaren calls 'spiritual friendships'[8] with friends at work, neighbours and people attending church community projects.

Publicity   There is one more way that our churches are present in our communities, and that is through the publicity that we might create and distribute to let people know that we are there. Several churches known to us have started to produce simple community newsletters full of human interest stories, plus details of what's on in the life of the church – especially featuring events of interest to non-members – and each time they distribute them they get positive feedback from their community.[9]

We admit it: newsletters have no great proven track record of bringing new disciples to birth. However, in times when the church has slipped off of most people's radar screens altogether, a well-produced news sheet pushed through the letterbox at least has the value of maintaining some kind of profile for the Christian community in the local community's eyes.

So whether it is through personal relationships, presence-in-the-community events or just well produced publicity, the church – like Jesus – needs to meet people where they are. But where do you go from there?

3. Integration and Information

Whilst it is true that Jesus was often in 'Go' mode, making incarnational connections in the fields, villages and beaches of Galilee, as Philip noted in chapter 5 at other times Jesus was in 'Welcome' mode, accepting crowds of interested onlookers at the edges of the discipleship group.

---

[8]   See Brian McLaren, *More Ready Than You Realize: Evangelism as Dance in the Postmodern Matrix* (Grand Rapids, MI: Zondervan, 2002).

[9]   There are examples of good Community Newsletters on the Winning Ways website.

In Matthew 5:1–2 we read that whilst Jesus' teaching on the mountain side was aimed at his disciples, he also welcomed the crowds who were interested in what the Rabbi had to say. By the end of the sermon it is in fact the 'crowds' who were 'amazed at his teaching' (Mt. 7:28).

Evangelism by ear-wigging was fine as far as Jesus was concerned apparently (was this an early example of belonging before believing?).

Building bridges in the workplace, home and neighbourhood is essential. It is where Jesus started, but not where he finished. Jesus, certainly came to seek the lost (or so he claimed) and he sought them here, he sought them there, he pretty much sought them everywhere.

But seeking was only half of the outreach deal; saving was the other.

None of Jesus' lavish displays of grace should lead us to imagine that Jesus was uninterested in whether or not *perceivers* of his kingdom became *receivers* of his kingdom. He had come 'to seek *and* to save the lost' and like a woman who'd lost precious coins or a shepherd who'd lost even one of his sheep, he was determined to do all that he could to find *and to save* them. When his seeking failed to find a response in the sought, his heart was broken (Lk. 13:34, 19:41) but when a lost child of God came home there was a celebration party!

Jesus didn't try to work out in advance who would *receive* and who would merely *perceive*; in fact his kingdom-displays were breathtakingly indiscriminate. Ten lepers were healed but only one returned to give thanks; five thousand hungry people were fed with no request for payment or response; water was turned into wine for people who had never met Jesus nor appreciated what he had done for them. The kingdom for each of these appeared as a beautiful unsought gift, a surprise discovery of treasure in the field of life.

But once people turned to Jesus they were given ample opportunity to learn what making the shift from follower to disciple actually entailed. The willingness to accept all-comers at the fringes of the discipleship band inevitably included the chance for them to take in information about Jesus and discipleship.

Both of these movements in the ministry of Jesus need to be emulated in some ways in our church outreach programmes. We need to provide regular and appropriate opportunities for friends and neighbours who show interest in the 'incarnation' phase of our relationship to access the Christian community (integration) and to begin to learn more about Jesus and the privilege of knowing and following him.

Some will come to a church *service* – but not many. Even so, it pays to look at how well our services introduce people to Jesus as he is worshipped by his twenty-first century disciples. More are likely to be willing to attend some kind of *social* event – maybe based in a home or small group or maybe in a larger setting – as their first step towards integrating with the community of disciples. Beyond that, maybe, lies a willingness to attend a *seeker group* such as an Alpha course, where there will be some fairly direct giving of information about following Jesus.

We will give more practical suggestions for the way to join up these opportunities in the second half of this chapter, but for now evangelistic church leaders will note that the building of bridges, which allow interested non-believers to integrate and receive information about the faith, is a structural issue for which they are responsible.

4. *Inspiration*

So as we follow Jesus along the I-Road of outreach, we have started (and continued) in steady *intercession* for our engagement with the world; we have reflected on the ways in which we and the members of our churches *incarnate* the good news in the world of friends, work colleagues and neighbours; we have begun to think through how we build bridges that allow interested people to *integrate* with our Christian communities and be *informed* about following Jesus: we now take the next turn in the road to look at how we challenge them to consider where they are on the I-Road themselves.

Jesus was not afraid to challenge people to consider where they stood in regard to their relationship with him. There comes a time when people who have been involved in a process of exploring faith are helped to see whether or not they have crossed the border from non-faith to faith.

The believing-before-belonging position asks us to imagine that someone can 'belong' to the church before accepting Jesus as Lord. We do not believe that they can 'belong' in any real and biblical sense: however, they can certainly be welcomed and even to a degree integrated into church life whilst they explore the Jesus-is-Lord life from close quarters. If that is what is meant by 'belonging', fine.

People who have attached themselves to churches as part of a *process* of coming to faith – and maybe feel like they belong – are in fact helped in that process by being challenged to reflect on 'where they are at' in their faith journey.

Research has shown there is no difference in terms of long-term commitment between people whose conversion is gradual and those who have a sudden 'crisis' conversion. Commenting on that research, Mike Booker and Mark Ireland reflect that 'what matters, it would seem, is not the speed of conversion but rather the certainty of convertedness (their word). The journey continues, but *the noting that at some point a boundary has been crossed is of fundamental importance.'*[10]

Helping people discover the boundary between 'seeker' and 'disciple' appears to be of great importance to their developing faith journey. This is where the equipping of every-member-missionaries to be able to help their contacts to understand boundary crossing moments is vital.

And it may also well be where the evangelist as 'individual preacher' (remember her from chapter 2?) still has a crucial role to play.

Certainly in the church that I led, I valued the integration of the preaching evangelist into the preaching programme of our church's life. As an 'evangelistic pastor/ teacher leader' (you need a wide office door for that job description) I felt that I was well able to help people along the process evangelism path; but I also knew that friends of mine (including Philip), who had the evangelistic gift, were inspired by God to draw people across that boundary between being sought and being saved.

5. *Initiation*

Here's where we return to the start of chapter 7: the need to make disciples. Someone, having journeyed with us as a church for a while, has made their decision and responded to the invitation to live as a disciple of Jesus themselves. Brief moment of celebration followed by more reflective panic. Now what do we do?

Of course, if you are all set up to regularly see seekers get saved, followers become disciples and belongers become believers, then you just trip the church 'follow-up' switch and the small avalanche of new Christian mentors, first-step

---

[10] Mike Booker and Mark Ireland, *Evangelism: which way now?* (London: Church House Publishing, 2003), p. 6, emphasis added.

discipleship courses and DIY devotional resources comes crashing to your study door. On the other hand ...

Making safe provision for the care and nurture of newborn children is perhaps the most important task of new parents. Maybe your church is all set up for individual or multiple new births but if not, how about asking a few people (including the newest Christians you can find) to get together to formulate a strategy for receiving new members into the family of your congregation?

There are plenty of resources out there, so again we are going to resist the temptation to be too prescriptive here. However, there are some resources that we have prepared which you will find detailed in Appendix C.

Joining it all up

Intercession; incarnation; integration and information; inspiration; initiation: the I-Road of Jesus-style outreach. One challenge remains: how do we join up all of these independent 'I's' into a unified whole-church outreach strategy, which functions as the organizational core of the culture of outreach that we are trying to create?

I imagine that none of the 'I's will be new territory for you. Even if you have never thought of yourself as an evangelistic leader, you have probably prayed for your community, maybe run an incarnational community activity from your church or even organized an Alpha or other seeker course. However, at the organizational level, what separates the evangelistic leader from the local pastor is that the former devotes themselves to strategically planning an outreach strategy that joins up these various pieces – *and they do that as the first act of forward planning in church life.* Constructing the I-Road first by forward planning key evangelistic events, prayer meetings, training courses etc means that the whole of church life rotates around outreach.

Perhaps you identified with the image that Philip drew in chapter 2 when he referred to a conversation we had with church leaders who were running lots of 'stepping stone' activities but recognizing that not only were some key stones missing from the river but that those they had put in place had been thrown in as random and didn't connect all the way from one bank to the other.

As you look at the diagram (below) of the various elements of Jesus-influenced outreach strategy that we have described, you can see that the arrows are very important in joining everything up. Without them, you just have the unconnected stones – or to change the metaphor – various loose planks in a bridge between your non-Christian contacts and their initiation into the first steps of Christian discipleship.

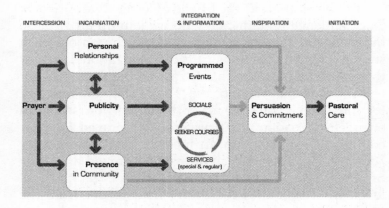

It's absolutely crucial to think through not only the individual elements themselves, but the way they strategically *connect*. The stronger the connections – the larger the arrows, if you like – the more effective your strategy will be. Joined Up Thinking is the secret to Third Circle effectiveness: random events and outreach hotspots just do not have the same impact as a carefully thought through strategic process.

Laying things out visually, as in our diagram, helps evangelistic leaders think through all the connections necessary for the process to work. By maximizing the joined-up nature of our programme, we can multiply its effectiveness radically. It's not simply about working on the individual elements themselves, but rather thinking through systematically how one element can lead to the next.

This is excellent news, because it means that most churches have greater evangelistic potential than they realize. The essential elements are often already in place. All that is needed is some work on the *connections*, so that disconnected activities unite into a holistic process.

Ask yourself – how does prayer connect with presence in the community? Is there appropriate and attractive publicity available for people to use with their friends to point them towards the programmed events? Is there a logical flow between our socials, our services and our seeker courses? Are we effective at moving people naturally from the information stage to the inspiration phase? What are our strategies here, how are we facilitating this, what training are we giving to make sure this happens, have we thought through the challenges and prerequisites? Crucially, do we have clear, coherent and fool-proof systems for nurturing and discipling new believers, no matter how or where they come to faith?

You'll notice that not all 'connections' are created equal. Some of the arrows in our diagram are bold, while others are light. This is a simple acknowledgement that there are things that we can take responsibility for, and there are things that only God can make happen. This is not a heartless marketing exercise, a matter of cynically placing people in a faceless disciple-making machine. Evangelistic leaders have to sow, and water, but ultimately it's only God that can cause the seed to grow.

So how can church leaders practice Joined Up Third Circle Thinking? It's all about planning, preparation, delegation and communication.

Planning   At the heart of the outreach map is the cycle of social events – seeker services and seeker courses. I used to routinely plan at least a year ahead and place these in the church calendar before anything else, using existing 'high days and holidays' as much as possible.

Even in post-Christendom, the legacy of Christian festivals remains in our yearly calendar. Christmas and Easter holidays are not just religious but secular holidays. It makes sense for the church to use this communal memory while it still exists and so positioning 'special guest services' at points where people outside the church may have some latent Christian leaning makes sense. Some leaders though prefer to avoid these all together and use other events in the social calendar to link their guest services to (world cups, Wimbledon or the Proms for example) or life-events (celebrating the birth of a child or remembering deceased loved ones).

Whatever 'occasion' the guest service is linked to, many people will be very nervous of attending a church service or be very cynical about what they will experience when they do. Therefore it is helpful to make it easier for them by making sure that your social event just predates your guest service – and that invitations for your guest service are available at the social event.

Thinking on from the guest service, it could be that some of the guests (who will almost exclusively, of course,

be friends of church members who they have been praying for – people bring people, right?) could be interested in attending a seeker course such as Alpha. It makes
a lot of strategic sense therefore if when you plan your
guest service and preceding social event, you also plan
in a seeker course to follow (making sure of course that
the course publicity is already printed and available at
both the preceding social event and the guest service
itself.

This seeker-bridge social event – guest service – seeker
course was something that I constructed two or three times
a year. The church calendar thus began with something
like the diagram on the following page already in place.

Of course, few people ever used the bridges as neatly as
they are laid our here. Often people would come to loads of
social events before trusting us enough to come anywhere
near a guest service or Alpha course – but because we
had planned ahead they always had an invitation to the
following events and eventually some responded.

Perhaps one of the most valuable aspects of creating
this series of bridges was that church members were clear
about where the main access points into experiencing
the church community were. As they developed their
'spiritual friendships' they were prayerfully seeking
the time when their friends might be open to taking a
first step onto one of these bridges. The opportunity was
clearly there for all of us in the church to use the bridges
that had been built, and if they didn't suit our friends, to
suggest additional planks to put in the bridges next time
we built them.

Everyone who organized any kind of group outreach
event within the church was also encouraged to fit in
with the cycle of core outreach activities planned. One
guy used to organize men's events which was great (don't
you love it when people volunteer to organize outreach

Feb	Mar	Apr	May	Jun	July	Aug	Sept	Oct	Nov	Dec	Jan
????	Socials	Easter Guest Service	Post-Easter Alpha starts		Small Group Socials		Socials and Guest Service	Alpha starts	Socials	Christmas Guest Service	Post-Christmas Alpha starts

activities?) However, asking him to make sure that his event preceded a church social meant that effectively he was putting another plank in the bridge – but putting it in at an appropriate point to maximize the potential of the whole church's programme. In that way the 'additional events' that always seem to crop up (knitting circles; Jive Sessions, etc) all have their outreach potential maximized, rather than just being a random stepping stone thrown in the river.

With the planning of key outreach events done, you can turn to the next core task: preparation.

Preparation

Three things head the list here, and we've mentioned them all already: people, publicity and prayer.

Now that your programme is set, it's time to schedule in the training that is required to equip every-member-missionaries to share their faith naturally in their neighbourhoods and networks. You could decide to do this in a *sermon series*, in a *special course* or in existing church *small groups*.

People It was my experience that, at least once a year, it was good to offer some kind of training input to the church to keep the issue of personal faith-sharing clearly on the church agenda. It was usually the next thing I put on the calendar. (See Appendix C for information on the Winning Ways equipping course and other resources.)

Publicity The next thing to get schedules was the deadlines for all of the invitations, press releases, posters, community newsletters, etc that we needed to produce in order to be able to promote our outreach activities in good time.

Prayer The production of prayer guides for the church outreach programme also needs to be pencilled in – as does any special prayer meeting – ideally just before the main outreach activities bridges take place.

This will develop your year planner to look something like the diagram on the next page.

Once this is in the calendar you can see what else you've got time to do. But two more important tasks remain.

Delegation Even with our simple model, it's clear that there's a lot of work to do here. That's why it's important to have a key leader for outreach identified on the senior leadership team who can take the initiative and develop the big picture.

From there it's an obvious move to involve the grass-roots evangelistic leaders that you identified in the first part of the book in the creation and execution of this programme. They may have had most of the great ideas and may be willing to put in the work required to make them happen.

You'll also want to develop the involvement of as many of your 'every-member-missionaries' as you can by approaching people and asking them to contribute their gifts to the outreach cause. Desktop publishing skills? Great, we've got just the job for you. Musician? Fantastic, start thinking about the special guest services or a cabaret night social. Cook? Wonderful, how about helping at the Alpha course? Donkey trainer? er ... right, let's think Palm Sunday guest service here.

Apart for the obvious releasing of spiritually gifted people into this programme, there are some other gifts that you may need to support you. We are not assuming that every evangelistic leader is good at strategic planning. If you are not gifted in that area (if you're not and you've read this far, we're impressed!) it would be

Feb	Mar	Apr	May	Jun	July	Aug	Sept	Oct	Nov	Dec	Jan
???	Socials	Easter guest service	Post-Easter Alpha starts		Small group socials		Socials and guest service	Alpha starts	Socials	Christmas guest service	Post-Christmas Alpha starts
						Outreach prayer meeting			Outreach prayer meeting		
							Teaching series on faith-sharing starts				
				Print all invitations, etc for Sept–Oct bridge events				Print all invitations, etc for Nov–Jan bridge events			

a prize asset for you to discover someone who has got those skills and can work alongside you to make this thing happen. Project manager? Praise God: I've got just the role for you.

Having planned, prepared and delegated there remains just one important task:

Communication   With all of this exciting programme taking shape, it is vital that the bridge structure and all that is involved with it is communicated to your church. This structure is the 'skeleton' of your culture of outreach. It means that you'll be talking about some aspect of outreach almost every time you meet as leaders and as church. It means that your budget will be leaning towards outreach activity. It means that your members will be equipped to share their faith and provide the stepping stones for their friends to use. All the pieces are joined up – you just need now to make sure that everyone knows about it.

In newsletters, Sunday notices and services, church websites, the pastor's blog, home group bulletins – in all of the communication channels you have – keep your joined-up outreach strategy on people's radar screens. Don't bore them with the structure itself (lots of people find structure a turn-off:) but *do* keep talking about the exciting and important things that are just over the horizon of church life – and *do* keep communicating any good news that arises from events that you have run.

Don't forget, the key to good communication is not intensity but consistency. It's in the cumulative effect of consistent communication that culture is formed and consolidated.

We hope that you can see the inherent potential in using this simple approach to structure your church outreach. We've given you a template for one particular approach, but you can adapt the joined-up model to your own particular situation.

It may be that you don't do guest services, per se, but have a philosophy of making every service inclusive. In that case, the questions to think through are exactly the same. How easy is it for people to connect the friends they're reaching out to with a church service? Do you have appropriate publicity available at every point of incarnation in the community? What are the mechanisms for helping visitors take the next steps along the information (and inspiration/initiation) super-highway?

Equally, you may not use a seeker course like Alpha, but nonetheless you need to consider just how you move people from the incarnation stage of community activities (parents and toddlers, youth groups, football club) into the integration and information phase, and so on.

When seekers engage with any one element of church life, it should never be a static experience. Rather, it should be like stepping on to one of those special 'travelators' you get in airports. Without having to work too hard, a natural system effortlessly carries them to the next 'gate.' Events should flow into one another, easily and obviously, rather than standing in splendid isolation from each other.

Joined-Up Third Circle Thinking

As you try to outwork some of the principles in this book, do remember that they are just that: principles. Don't let any specific ideas we may have given become straitjackets or whips for self-flagellation. Be creative; break the rules; go off-road. But in all of your creativity and adventure, don't lose sight of the core values of creating a culture of outreach in your church.

Strive to be an evangelistic leader who empowers grass-roots evangelistic leaders that in turn mobilize every member for mission. Keep paying attention to the core health of your discipleship-making programmes and your community-forming habits. Join up your outreach strategy: pray, plan, prepare people, delegate and communicate.

When we started this book we reflected on the projected future of the church in this nation. Statistics tell us that things are bleak. Churches are declining, and indeed closing, at an alarming rate. The cooling in credibility of the church and the loss of confidence in sharing good news seem to be inconvenient truths.

Yet for all that, we have hope for the church; we see a different future. It's our conviction that as church leaders grasp the vision to lead evangelistically and to create cultures of outreach, we could see a new wave of Christ-like outreach impact our nation.

We believe that, in the words of our Master, the fields are indeed ripe for harvest. The good news is still good news, and people are still looking for answers and for spiritual reality. A culture of outreach is one where Christians rediscover the power of the attractive community; where outreach becomes a natural part of every day discipleship, where people play to their strengths and present Jesus by lovingly serving the needs of those who don't know him.

Culture is all about a set of values becoming ingrained into the psyche of a community. It's about the right behaviour becoming a natural part of who we are, the way we do things round here, an instinctive, unconscious response. It manifests itself in unexpected and creative ways. It's organic, holistic and self-sustaining.

A culture of outreach isn't about a pre-packaged set of answers, or an off-the-shelf solution, but about leaders obeying the Timothy injunction to 'do the work of the evangelist', empowering and releasing the gifts and potential of the body. It's about engaging evangelistic gift at grass roots and using that to influence the whole body. It's about helping people discover how to be fruitful as every-member-missionaries, winning people to Christ through life-on-life incarnational investment. It's about aligning the programmes and activities of the church in a thought through way, so that everything joins up to give people the best possible chance of becoming disciples of Christ.

Our outreach needs to be turned on its head. Instead of starting with programmes and professionals, we need to start with people and nurture a process. As individual members are engaged as workers in the harvest, the questions move away from 'Here is our outreach structure, who can we put into it?' and move to 'Here are those that we are building bridges with, those that are asking questions and being drawn in – how can we structure an effective response?'

Over the last few years, as we have developed this material, and worked it through in many different real life situations, it's been our joy to witness ordinary leaders succeeding, members being mobilized and churches growing. It's our prayer that in your own situation something of what we've written here would be helpful, encouraging and stimulating. That you would see real, long-term, sustainable growth in your church.

May you share in the compassion of the Lord of the harvest. May you know the encouragement that the harvest is plentiful. And may you be inspired and enabled to see an effective release of ordinary, everyday workers in to his harvest field.

Questions for leaders

1. *Intercession*

- Are we covering every element of the outreach process in prayer?

- Is prayer for the lost present at every level of our gathered church life? Is prayer for non-believing friends a regular feature of every small group gathering, including our leadership team?

- How can we ensure that our outreach prayer remains creative, vibrant and inspirational?

2. *Incarnation*

- Are our members being encouraged and equipped to share their faith naturally with friends?

- Do we produce attractive and appropriate publicity for our church and events?

- Are we building bridges with our community through activities that serve real needs?

3. *Integration and information*

- Do we have a diverse portfolio of events in church life from purely social to deliberately evangelistic? How effectively and intentionally do they flow, and 'feed into' one another?

- Are our public meetings reasonably accessible to visitors? What might we need to do differently in order to be more accessible?

- Do we always make sure that there are suitable take home materials for guests at all of our events?

4. *Inspiration*

- Is every member of our church equipped to bring friends to faith?

- Do we use the gift of the evangelist effectively in our outreach programme? Do our presentations have that cutting edge?

- Do we make provision for people to come to faith in the context of our community activities? Do we need to think through appropriate ways of facilitating this?

5. *Initiation*

- Do we have clear and simple procedures for following up and nurturing new converts into the church?

- Is our nurture strategy centred around church structures, or is it flexible enough to fit around the life of the individual new believer?

- Have we made sure that all our members are able to disciple new believers, as well as reach out to non-believers?

Appendix A

Leadership Resources

As part of their long-term investment in local churches, David Lawrence and Philip Jinadu have developed some key resources for senior leadership teams.

Winning Ways leaders consultation

This is the main resource for leaders looking to develop an evangelistic leadership style and culture of outreach in their churches. The consultation gives an overview of some of the principles outlined in this book, and then allows a leadership team to perform a simple self-audit of their church. The audit provides a graphical representation of the church's areas of strength and weakness, both in terms of basic health and also evangelistic strategy.

Currently the consultation is available as a Leaders' Day with either Philip, David or a member of their team. It is also more widely available, however, as an online self-assessment programme.

The consultation covers three basic areas

1. Building healthy church
   - Establishing the key parameters of healthy church
   - Examining the findings of contemporary research

- Assessing your own church health through a guided questionnaire
- Discussing your findings and responses

2. Shaping strategic outreach
   - Reflecting on Joined Up Third Circle Thinking
   - Evaluating the effectiveness of your own church outreach programme
   - Discussing findings and responses

3. Engaging key people
   - An overview of the Church Growth Academy
   - How to select grass-roots evangelistic leaders
   - The role of a key leader for outreach
   - Sample plans for strategic outreach

For more information, or to access the online consultation, please visit

www.winningwaysweb.com

Leaders papers

The Winning Ways team have also produced a number of special leadership papers and reports on the outreach process.

Topics include:

- Running effective guest services
- A step-by-step guide to constructing a strategic outreach plan
- How to maximize the impact of social events

For more information, please visit

www.winningwaysweb.com

Appendix B

Church Growth Academy

The Church Growth Academy (CGA) was developed by Philip Jinadu and the evangelistic agency, ICQ, in order to provide a development process for grass-roots evangelistic leaders.

CGA comprises a mix of teaching, peer mentoring and on-the-job training that is typically carried out over an eighteen-month to two-year period. Delegates in any given church are overseen by a 'key senior leader' who has particular responsibility for outreach in the church. The teaching is designed to stand alongside a system of evaluation, reflection and practical outworking in church life.

The syllabus is divided into three core sections: Learning principles of effective outreach, Leading others in the outreach process and Training small groups in effective outreach.

There are sixteen keynote sessions, which are augmented by more reflective, local church driven, planning and feedback sessions. The topics are:

Learning principles of effective outreach

- Principles of lifestyle outreach
- Understanding church health
- How does salvation work?

- The power of a social
- Social action and outreach

Leading others in the outreach process
- Creating a culture of outreach
- Planning an effective outreach strategy
- Helping a group play to its strengths
- Sustaining the process long term
- Developing your leadership abilities

Training small groups in effective outreach
- Dealing with difficult questions
- Nurturing and discipling new believers
- The role of the Holy Spirit in outreach
- Communicating faith creatively
- Creative prayer
- Leading someone to Christ

Academy teaching sessions, featuring both Philip Jinadu and David Lawrence, are available on special studio-produced DVDs, complete with notes and application resources. There is also a library of small group outreach resources, outlining creative ideas and options for each month of the year. Teaching sessions are also available through a special internet podcast, as well as an online community discussion forum for delegates to submit questions, swap stories and request prayer.

For more information on how to access the Church Growth Academy please go to

www.churchgrowthacademy.com

or alternatively visit

www.winningwaysweb.com

Appendix C

Courses and Resources

Over the years we've developed a number of courses and resources for creating a culture of outreach in local church. This is an overview of two of them – a lifestyle outreach equipping course, and a new believers nurture course. You can use this outline to as a starting-point in devising your own resources. Alternatively, you can visit www.winningwaysweb.com for information on how to get hold of the courses themselves.

Winning Ways equipping course

This course is designed primarily for small group use, and is best delivered by your 'grass-roots evangelistic leaders' within an ongoing context and wider church strategy.

The course runs over five sessions and is intended to help kick-start a culture of outreach in a particular group. It uses a combination of DVD teaching segments (from Philip Jinadu) alongside Bible study, group discussion and practical application. The course includes Leaders notes and work books for each member.

This is an overview of the goals and content for each of the five sessions. Each session introduces and develops a key truth.

Session 1: How do we get started?

> *Setting the scene and debunking
> the myths*

- Goals: engage people with the course and teaching. Get people to talk honestly about hang ups and show a way forward. Outreach is a biblical imperative, but there are also natural biblical models for us to follow.

- Key truth – people bring people, relationships are the key.

Session 2: How do we build bridges?

> *Understanding how and why to
> build bridges, and with whom*

- Goals: get people to look clearly at their networks of relationships and begin to understand how to reach those around them. Effective personal outreach centres on getting close to people, meeting their needs and helping to break down barriers between them and Christ. Again, Jesus is our ultimate role model and it is his teaching and practice that we want to understand and emulate.

- Key truth – love people through a process, one step at a time

Session 3: How do we pray without getting bored?

> *Praying through a process and dealing
> with obstacles to faith*

- Goals: get people to talk honestly about hang-ups and issues with praying for non-believing friends. As people understand the principles of praying through a process, they need to identify where their friends are at spiritually now, and what things are holding them back. We want people to not only understand the concepts, but to commit themselves to regular prayer for specific friends with a sense of faith and expectation.

- Key truth – to be truly effective, pray people through a process

Session 4: How do we prepare hearts?

Understanding the importance of getting the ground ready for seed

- Goals: get people to look at their lives and priorities and make space to love people into the arms of Jesus. Sowing seed is a fruitless exercise unless the groundwork has been done. We need to discuss in practical terms how we can enter the lives of our friends. We also need to decide how we can engage friends in our lives, and be visible as a community of faith.
- Key truth: prepare hearts to receive the message, by building relationships that enter and engage.

Session 5: How do we move forward?

Ideas, principles and action to take things further

- Goals: to explain how the church outreach pro-gramme holds together and how we can make the most of it. To begin to plan and brainstorm some simple events for the group. Understanding that communicating God's story can happen directly and indirectly. Ultimately we want to move forward significantly in establishing a stronger culture of outreach in the group.

- Key truth: go and tell, Come and see – Share good news appropriately

Being a 'kick-start' course, the aims of Winning Ways are to introduce lifestyle changes and develop an outreach culture, rather than to provide an exhaustive evangelistic programme. It is therefore designed to be taken in conjunction with the teaching and training programme of the Church Growth Academy (Appendix 2). These five sessions in particular are helpful to follow on from the basic Winning Ways course, as and when appropriate

- Creative prayer
- Dealing with difficult questions
- The role of the Holy Spirit in outreach
- Communicating faith creatively
- Leading someone to Christ
- Nurturing and discipling new believers

'Up close and personal' new believers course
'Up close and personal' is a study book specifically designed to facilitate the discipleship of new believers. Although a new Christian can go through things on their own if they have to, the ideal scenario is for an older Christian – preferably the person who already has the relationship with them – to go through things with them, a bit at a time.

This resource, written by Philip Jinadu, draws on common experience and everyday analogies to teach the basics of the Christian faith. Ten foundational topics are covered using three basic questions – 'Why is this important?' 'What does the Bible say about this?' and 'How do I apply this to my life?' Designed to be worked through and adapted to the individual, 'Up Close and Personal' also features ten weeks' worth of daily personal Bible studies. Not only does it dispense teaching, it develops lifestyle.

The ten sessions covered are:

1. *God* (understanding the nature of God and how to respond to him)
2. *Cross* (how God's salvation story impacts and affects our life story)
3. *Prayer* (learning what prayer is and how to do it)
4. *Bible* (what the Bible does and how to read it effectively)
5. *Mission* (unpacking the Great Commission and our role in it)
6. *Church* (biblical images of church and what it means to be a part of it)
7. *Baptism* (what baptism means and how to prepare for it)
8. *Spirit* (the empowering impact of the third person of the Trinity)
9. *Lifestyle* (understanding temptation and learning to live differently)
10. *Future* (recognizing and understanding God's plans for your life)

For more information on 'Up close and personal', including a downloadable sample chapter, please visit

www.winningwaysweb.com

Appendix D

Pondering My Gifts

(see chapter 8: Forming community)

This checklist of questions is best used in combination with a face-to-face meeting with someone wishing to identify how God's Spirit has equipped them to serve in the church and the world

❏ What is my passion?

   Is there anything I do that particularly motivates me to the point of making sacrifices to do it?

❏ What do I take pleasure in doing?

   What am I already involved in that I enjoy doing?

❏ What do others praise me for doing?

   What have others consistently thanked and affirmed me for doing?

❏ What has been prophesied over my life?

   Has anyone ever offered me some directive or affirming words that I believed were from God for me?

❑ What do I do that produces good fruit?

> What is the effect of the ministry opportunities I have had?

❑ What do I feel prompted to do (that I've never done before)?

> Have I developed an appetite for serving in a particular way or place?

❑ What did I do in the past that has lain dormant and is ready for renewal?

> Have I let some gift or ability lie fallow and is God nudging me about that?

❑ What would I love to do if the power of the Spirit fell on me?

> Just dream the biggest spiritual dream you could; what would it involve you in?

❑ Is there any gift that I pray for more often than others?

❑ What is practically possible for me?

> In terms of my current season of life, what is the best way of using my gifts?

❑ How would I describe the potential of my God-given personality?

> Does my temperament lead me towards people-work or background-work? Do I prefer attention to details or the big picture? Am I better suited to long-term situations or short-term commitments?

Do I work better in a team or alone? Do predictable routines light my fire more than unpredictable spontaneity?

❏ As I reflect on these questions I perceive that:

    ❏ The gifts I believe I have are ...

    ❏ The gifts I most desire are ...